SEEING AND BELIEVING

In grateful remembrance of our parents,

Victoria and Frank Kacmarcik Sr.

and Beatrice and Benjamin Philibert,

whose love and faith taught us to see and believe.

Frank Kacmarcik

Paul Philibert

Foreword by
Gerard S. Sloyan

SEEING
AND
BELIEVING

Images of Christian Faith

A PUEBLO BOOK

The Liturgical Press   Collegeville, Minnesota

A Pueblo Book published by The Liturgical Press

Design by Frank Kacmarcik, Obl.S.B.

The Scripture quotations contained herein, unless otherwise noted, are from the New Revised Standard Version of the Bible, © 1989 by the Division of Christian Education of the National Council of the Churches of Christ in the United States of America, and are used by permission. All rights reserved.

Library of Congress Cataloging-in-Publication Data

Kacmarcik, Frank, 1920-
  Seeing and believing : images of Christian faith /
Frank Kacmarcik, Paul Philibert ; foreword by Gerard S. Sloyan.
    p.   cm.
  ''A Pueblo book.''
  ISBN 0-8146-6126-2
  1. Catholic Church—Prayer-books and devotions—English.
  2. Christian art and symbolism.   I. Philibert, Paul J.   II. Title.
  BX2182.2.K3   1995   95-16123
  246'.55—dc20   CIP

Printed in the United States of America.

CONTENTS

FOREWORD

Five hundred years ago with the invention of movable type a new symbol
system was made available to Christians as to all in Europe. They
hailed it as a means to bring to the literate minority God's word attested
in the Scriptures. All alike welcomed the printed book as an advance in
the diffusion of God's word. Some in the burgher class, however,
began to set it in opposition, not to God's word proclaimed and commented on in speech, but to all non-verbal symbols of the unseen,
Triune God. The book of the world began to be misprized as a way to
speak of deity because its midwives were that newly despised class,
the philosophers and the artists. The art forms that had conveyed some
small measure of the divine immensity and glory began to be spoken
against as pagan symbols: in three dimensions, the ''graven images''
the Bible railed against. These non-verbal symbols of God's love for
humanity in sight and color, but strangely not in sound, have been
under siege in some Christian quarters ever since.

But still they speak.

The visual artist whose drawings illumine these pages opted in
youth to work in the stark and spare. The straight line is his best
friend. At times he will resort to the curve and the wave. His first move
is long and deep reflection on the biblical stories of God in relation to a
people espoused. Then come, one by one, pregnant sketches bearing
within themselves the biblical figures and events: the Exodus, the God
who is rock, the dove that is Spirit, the crucified Jesus. Sometimes the

artist will go outside the pages of the Book to come forward in the centuries. Then we get the gemmed cross, the cup receiving blood from Christ's side, the Christian altar. The sketches alone are nourishment for the soul for all who know the Sacred Page.

But some do not. Even those who do and know it well may welcome guidance.

The verbal artist whose words of guidance are on these pages has one important qualification. He knows the words of the Bible. Never presuming to tell the reader what to look for in the drawings—the reason why all art criticism fails—he engages in reflections of his own on the biblical realities the biblical symbols point to. The sketches speak apart from the words, the words apart from the sketches. As complementary they make a rich serving.

A heartening development of our time is that the Christians who have been uneasy with any symbols of God besides the Bible and song, and those of the West who have lived a religion of symbol at diminished strength, have together begun to recapture the sacramentality of the world. It is the only tongue God has with which to speak to us: persons, things, events; the vault of the heavens, the abyss and its creatures; fire and wind, drought and rain. Inspired prophetic persons did no more than give *them* tongue, all that we may know something of the One whose justice and love knows no bounds.

The monastic layman plies his craft as the sons of Benedict have done—daughters too—for centuries. The friar of the *ordo praedicatorum* preaches, this time on the page, as he was ordained to do. Together they provide a catechism of the Catholic Church of the oldest and richest kind: the Bible and the liturgy brought to life through the media that speak to the human eye and ear and through them to the heart.

Gerard S. Sloyan

INTRODUCTION

In the beginning was the Word . . .
  at the end there shall be Vision. . . .

For more than thirty years, the drawings of Frank Kacmarcik have been a formative influence in my own life of faith. When I was a young seminarian in the late 1950s, I first noticed his covers for *Orate Fratres,* a journal of liturgical theology that now goes by the name *Worship.* It was a happy coincidence of my spiritual needs and this artist's sensibilities. His style has always been spare. His work is able to strip away all but the bare essentials, and then to illuminate those essentials with graphic power. His drawings helped me to assimilate the meaning of the central mysteries of the Church's liturgical life. They provided a window which opened up a space of faith beyond words and stimulated my hope and imagination.

Recently I was able to propose this collaboration of drawings and essays to Frank Kacmarcik. It brings together thirty-two of his religious drawings with a text that aims to unpack the richness of these images. These drawings have deep roots in the text of the Bible, in the Church's liturgical seasons, and in the depths of the human heart. The power of the Church's rites is expressed with great immediacy here. These symbols speak of God's presence in the world.

This book is an invitation to feast your spirit upon the symbols of Christian faith. We live in an age surfeited with talk—even talk about religion. Many people are tired of hearing about Churches and God. This collection is presented in the conviction that symbols of religious truths still have the power to build a bridge between God's mercy and our search for life.

Wise religious teaching has always insisted that no words can do justice to naming the Love that stands behind all reality. Whether we turn to Isaiah ("God's ways are not our ways . . ." [Isa 55:8-9]) or to St. Thomas Aquinas ("we can only say what God is not, not what God truly is . . .")[1] or to other great teachers of the Christian religion, we will find that we are taught to retreat from imagining that we could ever control God by naming, describing, and explaining the mystery. Instead, holy wisdom leads us to a moment of reverent surrender where—positioned by the revelation that we have received—we place ourselves before the mystery, become still in spirit, and await the anointing of faith that marries our spiritual hunger to God's compassion.

The insistence on the transcendence (the "beyondness") of God helps explain the important role that visual appeals to faith can play. In the case at hand, the drawings depict or evoke moments of grace in the lives of the great figures of the Bible. They also illustrate important symbols in the life of faith, like water, bread, and candlelight. The Church uses these symbols in its ritual life to make contact between saving moments in our history of encounters with God and the need for salvation in our personal lives. When people are baptized, they are not just told about the mystery of God's saving action, they are bathed with water that communicates to their senses the penetrating power of the grace of the sacrament within their lives. Sacraments are sanctifying because we believe that they bring about the reality that they signify within our lives.

Symbols of faith please and nourish our spirits because they communicate truth in a way broader and sometimes deeper than words. Centuries before any recorded documents, people painted or carved symbols telling stories about their lives and their beliefs on stones and the walls of caves. Some of these, like the paintings at

Lascaux in France or Altamira in Spain, are elegant and beautiful in ways that still touch us today. Such symbols are our oldest witness to the interior life of our paleolithic ancestors. Human beings are naturally symbol-makers. We derive deep satisfaction from stating the truth about reality and about our place in the world. Symbols are still vividly important today, as the T-shirt industry indicates.

Symbol and Church

The words *symbol* and *Church* share a common source in the Greek language and a common tendency to unify and empower. *Church* comes from the Greek word *ekklesia,* rooted in the verb *kalein*—to call or summon. Church is a gathering of people summoned together to share a common truth and a common destiny. The New Testament makes it clear, especially in the letters of Paul, that the people who receive the gospel as good news are more important than any building within which they assemble: they, not the building, are Church—and Paul calls them the body of Christ.

They are where the Spirit of Christ dwells visibly now that Jesus has been called beyond this world and now that believers have been given the gift of the Holy Spirit. Church is an invitation to find solidarity, harmony, and strength in sharing the gift of Jesus' Spirit. People are called to be Church in order to find an abundance of life and intimacy with God which they cannot attain on their own.

The word *symbol* also comes from the Greek. *Sym-ballein* means roughly throwing together or integrating elements that had been broken apart. *Symbol* is a mysterious word, since it functions as an indicator of dynamics that cannot be expressed fully in words. Symbols invite thought and stimulate reflection and utterance, but arise before words and run deeper than reflective thought.

Symbols preside over a marriage of desire and experience that gives birth to language and explanation. Yet the process of moving from symbol to understanding takes time and attention. While many different elements of the Christian religion have been named *symbols* (including the creeds), for centuries the dominant inclination has been to use the term primarily for non-verbal (or, in the sense just explained, pre-verbal) elements of religion.

In this book, the drawings of Frank Kacmarcik are symbols of Christian faith in precisely this sense. They are non-verbal images that point to faith experience. Further they have the capacity to integrate experience, desire, feelings, understandings, and actions in the work of believing. Whereas different individuals would bring their experiences of the Holy to utterance in distinctly different ways, the same individuals can all be nourished by these symbols at a deeper level of experience. In this way, symbols are among the chief elements that function to gather people as Church. Although believers may differ in the manner in which they articulate their common faith, they are united in their experience of the foundational symbols of Christian faith. This book is about just such a repertory of symbols.

Words and Images

Words and images differ. Words organize our response to the sequence of conversation, interaction, and reflection. Words seek to control—not necessarily to control the behavior of others, but to arrive at clear lines of explanation of thought and understanding. Words link together to form arguments that result in the demand: ''Think this way!'' Words do have a capacity to mediate truth—to lead students or thinkers to arrive at clearer understanding. But words also incline toward dogmatism: we can too easily indulge in the conviction that if my thought leads me to understand things this way, it must lead others to do the same.

Years ago, a teacher of mine used a telling example. He said that any text is a bit like the sediment that falls to the bottom of a jar when the mixture of elements suspended in a liquid have time to settle down. A text is the product of a mixture which includes thought, history, action, circumstances, and cultural qualities. We imagine that the settled text is adequate for clear interpretation on its own terms. But, in fact, to properly appreciate the text, we must understand it in terms of the conditions from which it emerged; and for the text to have cultural vitality today, it must be mixed and shaken together with the historical and cultural elements of our own time.

Ritual texts are also like this. They represent the faith experience of believing communities in the past. But if we treat them as though their vitality were assured simply by receiving them on their own terms, without taking care to link and mix them with dynamic elements of our own life and experience, the results will be disappointing. Like any other texts, our religious rites must be brought alive by symbols of living faith, or they will collapse.

By contrast, images are tools not of control, but of surrender. If words are the organization of speech, images can be thought of as the orchestration of silence. They evoke presence; they reach beneath the dichotomies of logical distinctions. Images have an elusive, ambivalent quality that allows the mind to postpone disjunctive choices. Images are *both/and*, while words tend toward *either/or*.

Images have the power to go directly into our feelings and invite us to belong—to connect with our confusion and pain or our joy and expectation. Images are architects of synthesis, making it possible for us to link together a variety of themes and concerns into a stance of trust or hope or conviction. It is interesting that computer language now uses the term *icons* for symbols that give workers access to programs and functions that open up further possibilities for thought and action. Images have always served as a threshold to new possibilities.

Given this explanation, we might say that symbols serve as depositories of our unprocessed experience. The Church invites us to use the major symbols of our faith to link and bind together the opportunities and dead ends, successes and failures, and joys and sorrows of our lives. The symbols of faith provide meaning for our most challenging struggles.

The Energy of Religious Symbols

The good news of the Christian message is that God's love is the fountain of life out of which our lives and our world have emerged. God has made everything out of love and so everything in this world is a point of encounter with God. As Teilhard de Chardin said, ''God is inexhaustibly attainable in the totality of our action.''[2] The world is bound together by God's creative love.

Our race has repeatedly gotten lost within the complexity of the world. Unlike the Little Prince's attempts to catch the fox, our attempts to meet God cannot be motivated by the desire for control. God can only be met in friendship and love. We must wait both for our own spirit to be evacuated of violence and possessiveness and for God's Spirit to touch our vulnerable hearts.

Into a world attuned to control and domination, God sent the one we call the Word, God's Son. John's Gospel describes God's Son as ''the true light, which enlightens everyone'' (John 1:9); ''he came to what was his own, and his own people did not accept him'' (1:11). In what may be the most eloquent phrase of the New Testament, John continues: ''the Word became flesh and lived among us'' (1:14). Jesus is God in the flesh, the Lover-Creator of the world as brother. Jesus took the conditions of our human living into his life, and in doing so transformed them all into instruments of communion with God. Jesus accepted the vulnerability of our weakness, pain, loneliness, and mortality, as well as the vulnerability of our hungry, loving hearts. The symbols of our faith are the images that touch and mediate this transforming life that Jesus lived for our sake.

As we turn to dwell upon images that put us in contact with the mystery of God, we will find that they have extraordinary power to affect us. These symbols have the power to open our eyes to ways of hoping that we have not known or have forgotten. They strengthen us as we gaze upon their powerful imagery. Like the brazen serpent raised up at Moses' instruction when the Israelites were afflicted with snakebite on their exodus march through the desert, the symbols of our faith are also symbols for times of striving or affliction. They demonstrate that we are not alone. They exercise a subtle healing on us as we turn to them and gaze and wait and hope.

xiv

A Path to the Depths of Our Hearts

The symbols of our faith are meant to work their way into the deep structure of our minds and spirits, burrowing beneath conversation and explanations, moving us into a territory of stillness and expectation. Living by the symbols of faith means, to some degree, renouncing the need to know immediately how things will turn out, renouncing obsessive control over events, and renouncing the anxiety that tends to accompany uncertainty.

These symbols are, in their own way, anchors of conviction. They help us to reorient our personal energies, so that we learn to esteem more highly the eloquence of silence in the presence of the beloved Giver of life. By showing us how to withdraw from our compulsiveness, they likewise extend pardon and mercy to our anxious spirits. We learn through the symbols that God's love for us is more tenacious and far more effective than any efforts we can make on our own behalf.

Most important, however, the symbols of our faith are an invitation to intimacy. These holy signs are privileged possibilities for encountering deep within our minds and hearts the healing good news that ''[nothing] will be able to separate us from the love of God in Christ Jesus our Lord'' (Rom 8:39). God wants us to experience embrace, not distance; affirmation, not rejection; energy, not despair. When we learn how to enter the symbols, we meet there an abundance of goodness and holiness.

Learning to See

Frank Kacmarcik frequently says that people need education in visual literacy. Our culture surrounds us with bold visual appeals to raw appetite. Today people must *learn* to see fully and deeply the symbolic dimensions of nature and of the arts.

Many of our national parks sponsor ''nature walks,'' during which a ranger instructs participants to notice and pay attention to unusual forms of trees or plants, birds or insects, or formations in the rocks or the land. This is an education in seeing, given in the hope that seeing will develop within the participants a new level of appreciation for nature and a new way of living in harmony with and respect for nature. Often enough, experiences like this are enough to promote in young people a life-long love of the outdoors and concern for ecology.

For centuries, the Church supposed that its people would learn to see in doing the rites, by a kind of osmosis where Christian symbols could (as it were) seep through the membranes of knowing, feeling, and caring and configure the imaginative landscape of the believer. But that was before we had parish assemblies of eight hundred or a thousand people at a time, before the impact of the ritual drama of the Church's sacramental life paled by comparison with an endless stream of electronic broadcasts, and before the relation between the ritual presider and the mass of the people in the Roman Catholic Church was stretched so thin by shortages of ordained personnel. We exist in a situation far different from that of our grandparents, let alone that of our ancient forebears.

Happily, positive forces are at work today to enable contemporary believers to deepen their appreciation for the mystery of Christian faith. Some Roman Catholic dioceses have strong ritual and liturgical arts departments. Some good journals for the liturgical arts and music exist. And the Roman Catholic bishops' statement on the arts and architecture in the service of worship is a good summary of the fundamentals regarding the role of the arts in the service of faith in an incarnate God.[3]

In that same spirit, Frank Kacmarcik and I offer to the reader the pages that follow. We hope that they will nourish, inform, sometimes surprise, and invite a response of faith, helping readers to reorganize more positively their own experiences of divine goodness, of thanksgiving and praise, of wonder and of hope.

A Discipline for Learning to See

The images that appear on the following pages are not just illustrations of ideas or stories from the Bible and the Church's liturgy. Their strength lies in their capacity to evoke a mystery of faith with such suggestive depth that we can return again and again to find new insight or a refraction of meaning that responds to a particular moment of searching or need. The thirty-two symbols that are included here touch upon fundamental realities of faith that illuminate our existence.

The primary goal of these images is not enjoyment of the ornamental shapes or the simple elegance of the drawings. These drawings are rather an occasion to enter a moment of quiet, repose, and communication between the deeper realities of our lives and a world of grace. In another way, they are lessons of faith as well. Through working with these images, we are invited into a fuller appreciation of God's love and of our destiny to live in the power of God's Spirit. The discipline of shutting out ordinary distractions and entering the lines of force these images contain can serve to open doors to a more profound experience of Christian sacramental life.

Praying with the Images

Let me recommend a possible approach for taking advantage of these holy symbols. It is important to become still, to set aside concerns and preoccupations arising from our busy life, and to open our spirits to grace. This requires a process of withdrawing from the noisy, frenetic pace at which we live the greater part of our days and entering a silence and a peace that allow us to open up our spirits in wonder and reverence. What is desirable is a privileged moment of holy learning where the symbol can bridge the experience of God's love and our everyday concerns.

Find a quiet and comfortable place. It is best if it is visually quiet as well, that is, not near distracting colors or pictures or a flickering TV screen. Make it clear to yourself that you are going to take a period of time—twenty minutes, perhaps—to be still and to wonder. Open your mind and your heart to the divine goodness that is blessing you with life; pray, if you believe, for the Lord Jesus and for the Holy Spirit to enter your heart. Then breathe slowly and deeply three or four times and settle deep into your seat. Gaze at one of the images—enjoy its shape, its clarity, and the fascination of what it suggests. Read as much of the essay that accompanies the image as you need to give you food for thought. Allow feelings, memories, and ideas to arise from your mind: welcome them; do not judge or censor them. At the same time, welcome the sense of God's presence that may be without any feelings or images. Desire God to work in you during these times however God wills.

At some point, be comforted by the awareness that you and the holy energy symbolized by the image have come together in this moment of rest and of prayer. And finally, when you are ready to bring your time of reflection to a close, use the prayer at the end of the essay or some other prayer to ask for faith and understanding, to bless and thank God, and to offer your own life as a channel for the presence and energy of grace within your world.

Our Part in the Mystery of Ultimate Reality

This last point is an important one. As St. Paul's Letter to the Romans teaches, our lives are not idle projects of interest only to ourselves. ''We do not live to ourselves, and we do not die to ourselves;
. . . whether we live or whether we die, we are the Lord's'' (14:7-8). In Paul's view, the life, death, and resurrection of Jesus Christ has changed our world and changed the meaning of human history. God's life in the world today is made visible through the presence and actions of those who have died and risen again in Christ. We are asked to be those agents of new life with Christ.

The gospel calls us to use our energies positively in a world that invites passivity. Again in Paul's view and in the view of Christian faith, we humans are the consciousness of the creation, linked biologically and spiritually with the destiny of the world around us. The energies and riches of the cosmos come to self-conscious awareness in us—whether through science, work, poetry, or countless other forms expressive of our human creativity. ''For the creation waits with eager longing for the revealing of the children of God; . . . the creation itself will be set free from its bondage to decay and will obtain the freedom of the glory of the children of God'' (Rom 8:19-21). The destiny of the earth and the fulfillment of the earth's vocation to be a splendor in the eyes of its creator are linked to our mindfulness and our thanksgiving.

The spiritual teaching of Buddhism stresses the quality of ''mindfulness.'' This mindfulness is a discipline—the fruit of meditation—that makes one aware of the connections between all aspects of life and the gift-like quality of life itself. The discipline of symbolic awareness which I am proposing through learning from the symbols in this book is similar. Such awareness will teach reverence toward nature rather than manipulation of natural forces; it will give us an awareness of our being loved, gifted, and filled with blessings, rather than of loneliness. Symbolic awareness is foundational to a full Christian life of faith and worship.

As you become familiar with the images and reflections in the pages that follow, you will also become more conscious of the connections between powerful experiences in your past life and the religious meaning that they are meant to have. Everything that occurred in the earthly life of God's Son has enduring significance and remains an instrument of healing and grace for those who can believe in Christ. Just as Christ's living in this world was a journey that brought him to share all the painful dimensions of our human predicament, so our entry by faith into his life brings true enlightenment, healing, courage, and peace to us.

As we shall explore further in the pages that follow, the Church's most challenging message to us and to the world is transformation through divine love. The Son of God became human to bring us the gift of God's divinity. Just as we believe that God has become human in Jesus Christ, so do we believe that God is calling us to become divinized—made God-like—in faith and love. This is the point of the journey of human living; this is the mystery of these symbols of faith.

Bon voyage!

BEGINNINGS

Where were you when I laid the foundation of the earth?
Who laid its cornerstone when the morning stars sang together
and all the heavenly beings shouted for joy?

Job 38:4, 6-7

ALPHA AND OMEGA

Even before we think about the mystery of our origin and our destiny, God has enfolded us in love and invited us into intimacy. Carl Jung, the influential psychologist, carved over the entryway of his lakeside retreat the words: ''Whether invited or uninvited, God is present.''[4] It is impossible not to have a relationship with God.

God is after all just the human word we use to point to the mystery that everything we know about has been brought into being by a Reality more real than anything in our experience. We forget that *God* is not a personal name and that the sense of the term is necessarily loose and vague.

Ironically many people today approach the word *God* condescendingly (as, for example, a belief unworthy of mature, autonomous persons who are responsible for themselves). The word itself, however, is shrouded in mystery and illustrative of the human mind's incapacity to understand its own origin. Much of the world's hostility to the idea of God is rooted in cultural and political struggles between scientists and Church officials. Today we would label as ''fundamentalism'' the theological explanation given for the Church's condemnation of Galileo's scientific views in the sixteenth century.

Contemporary theologians no longer imagine that science must be considered hostile to revelation. But the same may not be true of many less sophisticated believers who cling to familiar images of God from their childhood without much opportunity to inform themselves

3

of advances in religious understanding in recent years. Some years ago a famous theologian shocked many ordinary believers when he titled his university lectures "The God Problem." But, in fact, "God" is a problem if we imagine that we understand the mysterious Reality enough to be able to speak on behalf of the Holy One. Real knowledge of God leads us to silence.

It certainly leads us to give up explaining God in ways that use the idea of God as a warrant for our own vision or ideas of the world. God and science are not in competition, even though too many believers and too many scientists seem to think the opposite. Furthermore, people otherwise quite disinterested in religion expect God to provide sanctions against those who offend their expectations for a tidy world.

An important step in spiritual growth is to acknowledge that we really don't and can't know much about God—certainly not much about what God is up to in our world or in our lives. We need to adopt a posture of awe and reverence: we need to be led into the arena of amazement.

A century ago, a German scholar named Rudolf Otto attempted to evoke a sense of this predicament of the human mind confronted with the idea of God. He suggested we may best name God as *mysterium tremendum sed fascinans:*[5] a fear-inspiring mystery—awesome and exciting—that attracts us and compels our interest. Otto's intent was to evoke the immensity of God as well as some realization that in talking of God we are talking about a reality that eludes our control or our powers of manipulation. Most believers could use a healthy dose of contact with the transcendence (the "beyondness") of God.

In the Book of Revelation we read, " 'I am the Alpha and the Omega,' says the LORD God, who is and who was and who is to come, the Almighty" (1:8). This passage near the beginning of the Revelation of John the Seer is a parallel to the powerful moment when God encountered Moses in the desert at the burning bush and revealed the divine name as "I AM": "Say to the Israelites, 'I AM has sent me to you' " (Exod 3:14).

4

God challenges our understanding of what a name is. In revealing God's name as "I AM," God alerts us that our capacity to reach out through a name to something so far beyond our experience is hopelessly limited. God's revelation proposes another name: God is Alpha—the beginning of the Greek alphabet—the beginning of those symbols by which we attempt to spell out our understanding; God is Omega—the last letter of the alphabet—the destination of our efforts to understand and express reality. Isaiah (44:6) records the Lord's words: "I am the first and the last; besides me there is no god."

In this imagery, God tells us that divine reality precedes us and perdures beyond our finite being in this world. God is our origin and our destiny. Put metaphorically, God is the source from which our life emerges and the sea of life into which our experience flows. At no point are we far away from God.

Psalm 139 poetically expresses this sense of God in our lives:

"O LORD, you have searched me and known me.
You know when I sit down and when I rise up . . .
Even before a word is on my tongue, O LORD, you know it
    completely. . . .
For it was you who formed my inward parts;
You knit me together in my mother's womb. . . .
My frame was not hidden from you, when I was being made
in secret, intricately woven in the depths of the earth."
                                                    (vv. 1-4, 14, 15)

God's knowledge of us is not the speculative, detached knowledge of a scholar who has figured something out. God's knowledge of us is the passionate, committed knowledge of the artist who is deeply engaged in the outcome of the craft.

St. Thomas Aquinas in the thirteenth century expressed in classic fashion a truth of Catholic theology that has always marked good theological understanding. We must understand our lives in terms of a leave-taking from God as the source of our being and a return to God as the ultimate meaning of our existence.[6] Aquinas saw human life as a

5

journey empowered by divine love and with a destiny to eternal love. He was not simplistic about it: he never claimed to fully understand the whole mystery of life. But the meaning of God for him was this vortex of primordial Love from which all reality emerged into physical existence and in which all reality finally finds its ultimate meaning.

In this sense, the symbol *Alpha and Omega* is a proper place to begin this set of reflections on Christian images of God. With Thomas Aquinas, we can try to understand that it is inconceivable for us to exist outside of the creative love of God. God's loving is the proper source of our being. At any moment we can be certain that we are loved and treasured by that nameless Abundance of Life whose avatar is Jesus Christ. God is Alpha—the beginning.

God is also Omega. Most people have moments when they wonder what life is all about. Even with loving companions, meaningful work, supportive communities, and many pleasurable satisfactions, we can find ourselves bumping up against feelings of emptiness and meaninglessness. Scripture is filled with examples. Psalm 139 again: ''If I say, 'Surely the darkness shall cover me and the light around me become night,'—even the darkness is not dark to you; the night is as bright as the day, for darkness is as light to you'' (vv. 11-12).

Invited or uninvited, as Carl Jung said, God is present. It is not so much for God's sake—to offer adoration and thanks—that we must learn to enter the mystery of this unfailing love of God. (God does not need our esteem in any sense like what we mean by ''need.'') Rather it is essential for the integrity of our humanity. For the Omega is not just an idea, but is rather the living energy that sustains us in being and, in doing so, witnesses to our value in God's eyes. The Omega point is our home-coming, our arrival back where we belong, our destination in the journey that is life-emerging-from-eternal-love. God wants us to know this, and to share our knowledge. God wants us to feel safe in the power of the One who is Alpha and Omega.

Gracious Giver of our life, sea of love, source of light:
You have endowed us with hearts hungry

6

for meaning, for love, for beauty, for friendship.
Awaken a deeper understanding within us that we are always
 united to you.
Help us to put aside names too narrow, images too small
 to contain your goodness and your care for us.
Within the embrace of your eternal power, we journey safely
 from birth to death to life again.
Let us know; let us understand; let us break open this good news
 like sweet fruit beneath the skin of every day's experience.

CREATION

"Praise the LORD, sun and moon
   and all you shining stars!
Praise the LORD, you highest heavens,
   and all you waters above the heavens!
Let them praise the name of the LORD,
   for God commanded and they were created.
God established them forever and ever;
   he fixed their bounds, which cannot be passed."
                                        (Ps 148:3-6)

Many people have found faith at the edge of the sea or gazing at the colors of a setting sun. Sometimes there is a strange harmony between the inner longing of our hungry hearts and the boundless abundance of beauty in nature. Some psychologists call this an "oceanic feeling"—the sense that one feels lost in and insignificant before an amplitude of being beyond our abilities to measure or to grasp. When such a moment is perceived as beauty and goodness, our reaction is one of gratitude and adoration for the hidden Giver whose power brought forth such a gift.

   St. Paul in his Epistle to the Romans argues that everyone should be able to understand God as the primal source from which reality comes forth. "Ever since the creation of the world his eternal power and divine nature, invisible though they are, have been understood and seen through the things that he has made" (Rom 1:20).

9

Thomas Aquinas saw the relation between creatures and the Creator even more graphically; in his view, God not only brings reality into being, but sustains reality by loving it and providing for it. In his thirteenth-century Latin wording, he calls this *conservatio*—upholding the world in being.[7]

The Book of Genesis is a narrative about the beginnings of things, aiming to make it clear that God is the origin of all reality. The words of Genesis are rich and poetic. By naming the coming into being of each aspect of the world we know, Genesis evokes a sense of the full scope of God's power and authority over everything that exists. God also becomes our role model for the function of work; for six days God goes efficiently about the process of completing the details of the creation. Then "God blessed the seventh day and hallowed it, because on it God rested from all the work that he had done in creation" (Gen 2:3).

When it comes to the creation of humankind, we see a particularly intimate image of God's care. "Then the LORD God formed man from the dust of the ground, and breathed into his nostrils the breath of life; and the man became a living being" (2:7). The human creature is crafted so as to be a vessel for God's breath or spirit. This creature who will "have dominion over the fish of the sea and over the birds of the air and over every living thing that moves upon the earth" (1:26) is composed of the lowest element imaginable and the highest reality imaginable. The human creature is composed of the dust of the earth (upon which we walk without thought of concern for it) and the Spirit of God the Creator. Humans will always have difficulty balancing the tension between these radically disparate elements of earth and spirit.

It remains true that the only condition under which we can sustain life is to take in again and again the breath of life. This ceaseless rhythm of breathing is a metaphor for God's equally incessant giving of life to us. Life is an on-going process: precarious, yet strong; developing, yet taken-for-granted. It is not so surprising, then, that breathing plays such an important role in the discipline of contemplative prayer. Contemplatives learn how essential it is for them to slow the pace of their activities and to tune out the distractions of their busy concerns so that they can respond to God's invitation in Psalm 46 to ''Be still, and know that I am God!'' (v. 10).

This active insistence on stillness by contemplatives not only removes distractions, but also serves to articulate our mute attention and to include within the work of adoration, praise, and thanksgiving all our bodily processes. That is how God made us to be. Every part of ourselves is meant to be engaged in prayer.

''Let us make humankind in our image, according to our likeness. . . . So God created humankind in his image, / in the image of God he created them; / male and female he created them'' (Gen 1:26-27). Like God, we are called to be mindful and lovingly protective of everything that is. But once we lose the link to God's own loving impulse of creation, we lose perspective on the whole enterprise of our extraordinary capacity to exercise dominion.

The theology of the first chapters of Genesis is a rhapsody to God's beauty and majesty. But this tone is perhaps wrong for our own life situation. Creation is no longer the same inspiring pastoral symphony stirring the heart to gratitude. We have grossly wounded creation with pollution, the poisoning of the earth, and the genocide of countless species now extinct because of the violent and mindless use of our ''dominion.'' Has God's word something to say to us about all this?

> ''The LORD answered . . . out of the whirlwind: . . .
> 'Where were you when I laid the foundation of the earth?
> Tell me, if you have understanding.
> Who determined its measurements—surely you know!
>   or who stretched the line upon it?
> On what were its bases sunk,
>   or who laid its cornerstone
> when the morning stars sang together
>   and all the heavenly beings shouted for joy? . . .
> Can you lift up your voice to the clouds,
>   so that a flood of waters may cover you?

Can you send forth lightnings, so that they may go
   and say to you, "Here we are"?
Who has put wisdom into the inward parts,
   or given understanding to the mind?' "
                                    (Job 38:4-7, 34-36)

As with Job, God's word addresses us and tries to shake us out
of our inattention. If we could hear that word in our deepest being, we
would understand that we and creation are one—one beloved gesture
of God's benevolence and beauty shared from the heart of Reality to
the limits of the cosmos. Perhaps in coming closer to creation's beauty
we will be able to achieve the profound transformation of spirit that
came upon Job: "I had heard of you by the hearing of the ear, but now
my eyes see you . . ." (Job 42:5).

Give us keen eyes and gentle hearts, Maker of all—
   eyes that can find your love in your gifts,
   hearts open to your lavish care.
How do we miss the messages that you send us
   in the clouds, the hills, the stirring leaves?
Your bounty speaks to us always of fullness and love.
We need to learn the lessons of seeing,
   tasting and savoring the strong, simple flavors of beauty.
"The heavens are telling the glory of God;
   and the firmament proclaims God's handiwork.
Day to day pours forth utterance,
   and night to night declares knowledge.
There is no speech, nor are there words;
   their voice is not heard;
Yet their message goes out through all the earth,
   and their witness to the end of the world."
                                    (Ps 19:1-4)

THE
BURNING
BUSH

Moses was wandering in the wilderness of Mount Horeb because he could get work only from his father-in-law as a shepherd. He was a political refugee, hiding out, homesick, and confused. Like shepherds everywhere, he was alone most of the time—a situation that prompts reminiscence and reflection. He had much to wonder about, including the strange and rich circumstances of his earlier life: being saved by the Pharaoh's daughter, given privileged access to Egypt's power structure, living a life divided between the royal elite and the enslaved Hebrew people from whom he came. Then he had to flee: in anger he slayed an Egyptian who was beating an Israelite, and this murder enraged the Pharaoh. He fled into the land of Midian, into the desert east of Egypt.

As things turned out, the fleeing Moses was resting by a well when the daughters of Jethro were accosted by shepherds in that place. Moses drove away the shepherds, watered the women's flocks, and became the friend of these people and the husband of one of Jethro's daughters. So in time this impulsive, energetic man found himself doing the least impulsive, least energetic work imaginable; he became the shepherd for Jethro's flock. Moses was drifting, "an alien residing in a foreign land" (Exod 2:22). In the midst of these unsatisfactory circumstances, he received a call destined to change the lives of his people.

While keeping the flock, Moses led them to a place called Mount Horeb, also known as Mount Sinai. "There the angel of the LORD appeared to him in a flame of fire out of a bush; he looked and the bush

15

was blazing, yet it was not consumed'' (3:2). Moses was drawn to approach this strange sight; he could not figure out what was going on. ''When the LORD saw that he had turned aside to see, God called out to him out of the bush, 'Moses, Moses!' And he said, 'Here I am' '' (3:4). The tables have been turned. Curious Moses deciding to explore an unusual phenomenon in an uninteresting situation suddenly becomes chosen Moses called by a voice that reaches into the depths of his being.

God immediately warns Moses of the power of the moment: he tells him to come no closer, to remove his sandals, and to know that he is standing on holy ground. ''He said further, 'I am the God of your father, the God of Abraham, the God of Isaac, and the God of Jacob.' And Moses hid his face, for he was afraid to look at God'' (3:6). Moses' former ambivalence, as a man of destiny who had lost his chance to use his gifts meaningfully to help his enslaved people, becomes a new ambivalence. For here he encounters the living God and is allowed an intimacy that no one since Adam has had, while at the same time he is brought to recognize the overpowering energy and majesty before him.

This moment is full of revelation, pregnant with significance. In the dryness of the desert, it is likely that a fire would quickly swallow up anything it catches—especially a thorny desert shrub. Yet here is a fire, seen from afar, that blazes without being consumed. Here is a symbol out of eternity, where there is no before or after, no corruptibility or diminishment. Here is a fire whose meaning is pure majesty.

God's voice tells Moses to bare his feet. This is reminiscent of the unguarded simplicity with which the man and the woman dwelt before God in their nudity before the fall—before shame. It is a reminder of the innocence which God bestows upon those called, not because they have justified themselves, but because God has called them into the divine presence and accepted them. Moses understands the meaning of this loving call from the Living One, and is immediately overwhelmed with feelings of inadequacy. He hides his face—in fear of God's power, in shock at this sudden revolution in his prospects.

So now Moses, who fled Egypt out of fear of reprisal for murder, is sent back to where he had often longed to be. Strong and impulsive

16

but also fearful and insecure, he is given a vocation to set his people free. He must go confront the Pharaoh—a new Pharaoh—and demand justice and liberation. He must be God's voice on behalf of his own people.

He protests, "O my LORD, I have never been eloquent, neither in the past nor even now that you have spoken to your servant; but I am slow of speech and slow of tongue" (4:10). But God insists: " 'Now go, and I will be with your mouth and teach you what to speak!' But he said, 'O my LORD, please send someone else!' " (4:12-13). What a moment of fear and trepidation—what ambivalence! Moses both wants to go and fears to go. Moses both desires to serve and feels inadequate. Moses is everyone who has ever been called to give a life in devoted service.

In the end, God sends Moses back to Egypt. All the pieces fall together in this strange wilderness encounter. Moses can now employ all he learned among the wealthy and educated, all the skills he learned at court, all his energy and all his impulsiveness. Moses can now also understand his weakness and his fear and act not out of arrogance but obedience. He learned essential lessons in Midian.

What is it about the desert? About fasting? About retreats? About being stripped of supportive and comforting props? God seems to find it easiest to get our attention there. God's revelation is eloquent not only in words, but in the extended silence of the burning bush, the smoking mountain, the hovering dove, the descending tongues of flame, and the bread broken and shared. Our whole being must receive the good news—our eyes and other senses as well as our thoughts.

The burning bush was on the site of Horeb—of Sinai. Moses would go back there with all the people and again would meet "I AM." Years later, the grieving prophet Elijah would retreat to this same place to pray and be strengthened; he would receive a visit from God as remarkable as that of Moses.

God told Elijah to stand on the mountain and await the Lord's coming. "Now there was a great wind, so strong that it was splitting the mountain and breaking rocks in pieces before the LORD, but the

Lord was not in the wind; and after the wind an earthquake, but the Lord was not in the earthquake; and after the earthquake a fire, but the Lord was not in the fire; and after the fire a sound of sheer silence. When Elijah heard it, he wrapped his face in his mantle and went out and stood in the entrance of the cave'' (1 Kgs 19:11-13).

Moses began his career as a prophet and Elijah ended his lifetime as a prophet by meeting the Holy One in the desert—one in the burning bush, the other in great stillness. Both will one day meet Christ on another mountain and finally let all their words—the words of the Law, the words of the prophets, and the words of the gospel—be superseded by a radiant cloud and a commanding voice.

> Lead us over and over again to remember
>   our own story of calls and encounters
>   with your holiness, Holy One.
> Make us understand that we have not learned your teaching
>   until our bones and our senses have been filled
>   with the radiance of your presence.
> Call us apart, like Moses and Elijah, and bid us to be still
>   to be stripped of masks and trappings
>   to be naked in truth before you.
> And let us see your eternity, your energy, your love
>   let us know your truth
>   in the blaze of fire that is never consumed.

JOURNEY
THROUGH
THE
WILDERNESS

"By faith Abraham obeyed when he was called to set out for a place that he was to receive as an inheritance; and he set out, not knowing where he was going" (Heb 11:8). So Abraham, who was called the father of all believers by Paul (Rom 4:16), serves as an example of trust in a God who can seem reckless in caring for friends. The theme of journeying is woven throughout the pages of the Bible, from Abraham's trek out of his homeland down to Jesus' itinerant preaching throughout Judea and Galilee. God keeps the elect on the go.

The human heart has to struggle between its urges for stability and its unpredictable restlessness. In early adulthood, the desire for travel and rich experience is strong. Impatience with the constraints of parental and institutional formation and with the familiar patterns of family and schooling promotes a thirst for novelty and for knowledge of the world. Yet sooner or later, most people settle down, form their own families, develop their own routines of work and society, and become attached to a new pattern of familiar behavior. Ordinarily most people will invest in stability, even if that means surrendering hopes and dreams. Stability offers us predictability and control—high values in our culture.

The Bible's stories of God's people, however, show us a different picture. God never lets the chosen ones of Scripture settle into a rut. All the important figures of the Bible are tested and matured through a journey. Like Abraham and Sarah, the ancients of the Old Testament were propelled into adventures that brought them in touch with circumstances that would radically change their lives. This was true of Jacob and Leah and Rachel, of Joseph and Asenath, of the great king David and his wives, of the prophets; it was true as well of the apostles. Such a journey is a profession of faith in God's will and guidance. The friends of God are never allowed to forget this lesson.

The great journey that symbolically summarizes the mystery of God's invitations to growth and new life is the Exodus. The Hebrew people, who came into Egypt at a time of famine with Joseph as their protector (Gen 43–50), settled down into the land where they later became slaves of the Pharaohs. God had to rouse them out of their complacency by sending Moses, Aaron, and Miriam to them. Eventually Moses convinced the Hebrews to set out for a promised land of liberation, and likewise convinced the Pharaoh after painful struggle and plagues and death to let them go. Such journeys are not taken lightly, they are not easy.

At the time of Israel's later exile in Babylon, the prophet Isaiah harkened back to the Exodus: ''Awake, awake, put on strength, O arm of the LORD! Awake, as in the days of old. . . . Was it not you who dried up the sea, the waters of the great deep; who made the depths of the sea a way for the redeemed to cross over?'' (Isa 51:9-10). The lesson remains for the ages: there is nothing that can impede the Lord's decision to act on behalf of the people. But, as in the time of the Exodus, the people must be awakened to a promise of deliverance from their misery and come to believe in God's promise of a new and fulfilling life.

The episode of the people standing with bewilderment at the edge of the sea with Moses at their head, fleeing from Egypt's army, establishes a pattern. Each life-changing journey will have its element of impossibility. There will be moments of not knowing how to return to a viable past or how to move forward against obstacles. But the Lord instructed Moses: ''Tell the Israelites to go forward. But you lift up your staff, and stretch out your hand over the sea and divide it, that the Israelites may go into the sea on dry ground'' (Exod 14:15-16). This moment is forever remembered.

Good navigation is essential for any journey. An important part of navigation is remembering where you have been and how you got to where you are. For those of us now on a path to some mysterious Promised Land, hinted at in our prayer and discernment, the discipline of remembering our past salvation journeys is as vital for our success as the remembrance of the Exodus was for the Hebrews. We can quickly forget the moments that were decisive for the paths we have taken. Equally we can easily dismiss the import of the special graces that have helped us choose. There are moments in every life meant to be stored up like treasure—nourishing moments that become energy for a life-time (cf. Luke 2:19, 51).

A discipline of great usefulness when one begins a relationship with a spiritual director or guide—a journey in itself—is to sort out the narrative of one's personal salvation history. It is beneficial to be forced to recall those graced moments when each of us experienced the special presence of God in our lives and felt a call to respond with generosity. We need to ponder the significance of God singling us out by the favor of a guiding grace.

When were those moments that changed our destiny? Who were the persons who helped us to see? Where were the places this happened? What books, images, occasions, and spaces were associated with these hours of destiny? All these details are personal symbols of God's power in our lives—signs of election, guideposts for freedom.

It helps, when one feels stuck, to recognize that God has cared enough to break and enter our hearts. Our passion for certainty can bring us severe pain in times of ambiguity. Yet each of us has only the hazy horizon of available reality to guide our journey. ''The path of the righteous is like the light of dawn, which shines brighter and brighter until full day'' (Prov 4:18). Until that bright dawn illumines our lives, the movements of our journeys are tentative and insecure. But ac-knowledging the context of a journey on which one is called out of psychic slavery and called forth toward freedom is a precious key. Given that adventure, one can put up with many inconveniences.

Perhaps the most dramatic example of a spiritual journey in the New Testament is Paul's conversion from observant Pharisee to Jesus-believing Jew. "Now as [Saul] was going along and approaching Damascus, suddenly a light from heaven flashed around him. He fell to the ground and heard a voice saying to him, 'Saul, Saul, why do you persecute me?' . . . 'Get up and enter the city, and you will be told what to do' " (Acts 9:3-6). Paul's journey was marked with the trauma of blindness. "For three days he was without sight, and neither ate nor drank" (9:9). Then a disciple in Damascus named Ananias came to him and lay hands on him and the Lord restored Paul's sight. Paul then saw everything in a new light.

Not all the significant journeys of our lives are forced upon us with comparable violence. A phenomenon of great interest in our world today is the growing incidence of volunteer service through agencies like the Peace Corps, or affiliate membership in mission-sending societies or religious communities. Such opportunities allow a person to achieve new perspective, cut loose from the burden of stale duties, and test possibilities for a freer and more generous life. Blessed are those who recognize the voice of the Holy One at the root of their restlessness and who make that voice the destination of their wanderings. They can make their own the cry of the psalmist: "You show me the path of life. In your presence there is fullness of joy; in your right hand are pleasures forevermore" (Ps 16:11).

> God, you have numbered the hairs of our head,
>   you know our ups and downs;
> you decipher our hidden thoughts more clearly than we ourselves
>   and take our burdens into your heart.
> This alone will you refuse us: to let us stagnate
>   or wilt or wither.
> Rather you call us further into life,
>   entice us to follow with abandon your own path

and so leave slavery behind
to become beacons of freedom and signs of life's fullness.
Open the sea: break through obstacles,
let our sight penetrate the gloom
that holds us back from life and generous love.
Our journey is clear to you:
call us again—and speak, Lord, distinctly.

COMMAND-
MENTS

During the nineteenth century, French sociologists began to use the term *anomy* to describe the situation of people who had lost their bearings within society. This emptiness affected many people during the French Revolution. The term is meant to sum up all the feelings of hopelessness and dead ends that were produced by the immense social changes of that time. People in the growing underclass of the unemployed, who seem to have lost all sense of belonging, are also examples of those whose lives are marked by anomy. This predicament is still with us.

Anomy comes from the Greek and means ''a lack of order,'' although the Greek word *nomos* is rich and signifies also law, meaning, and structure. Someone without *nomos*—someone in *anomy*—is living in great confusion, pain, and emotional isolation. Most people who suffer anomy feel powerless to do anything about their situation—which may be the worst suffering of all.

In order to understand what the ten commandments meant to the Israelites, we have to appreciate the situation of anomy which they were experiencing at the time when God reached down to them from Mount Sinai and gave them the tablets of the Law. They had endured generations of slavery under the pharaohs and lost their sense of dignity and destiny. They had started wandering in the desert on their way to a Promised Land that none of their party had ever seen. They were little more than a loose assortment of Israelites in Egypt and their sympathizers attracted to the worship of their God. They had no strong sense of unity or purpose and they already wondered if they had made a mistake in leaving Egypt, horrible as it had been.

"The people quarreled with Moses and said, 'Give us water to drink.' Moses said to them, 'Why do you quarrel with me? Why do you test the LORD?' But the people thirsted there for water; and the people complained against Moses and said, 'Why did you bring us out of Egypt, to kill us and our children and livestock with thirst?'" (Exod 17:2-3).

Into this chaos, God spoke words of love, order, commitment, and destiny. It would be a great mistake, then, to imagine that the commandments of God were received by the Israelites in the desert as a threatening burden that placed uncomfortable demands upon their free self-expression. They were recognized as *nomos*—law, meaning, structure, and destiny—for the chosen people.

"God spoke all these words:
I am the LORD, your God, who brought you out of the land of Egypt,
    out of the house of slavery; you shall have no other God before me.
You shall not make for yourself . . . idol[s] . . . You shall not bow down to
    them or worship them; for I the LORD your God am a jealous God. . . .
Remember the sabbath day, and keep it holy. Six days you shall labor and
    do all your work. But the seventh day is a sabbath to the LORD your
    God; You shall not do any work. . . . For in six days the LORD made
    heaven and earth, the sea, and all that is in them, but rested on
    the seventh day; therefore the LORD blessed the sabbath day and
    consecrated it.
Honor your father and your mother. . . .
You shall not murder.
You shall not commit adultery.
You shall not steal.
You shall not bear false witness against your neighbor.
You shall not covet your neighbor's wife;
You shall not covet your neighbor's house . . . or anything that belongs
    to your neighbor" (Exod 20:1-17).

28

Three precepts command honor and service to the Mystery of Life who is our source and our destiny. Seven precepts command justice and respect for the creatures of this world. All ten bind us into a covenant of mutual attachment: "I shall be your God and you shall be my people."

God's appearance on the mountain was an unmistakable sign of power and favor. "When all the people witnessed the thunder and lightning, the sound of the trumpet, and the mountain smoking, they were afraid . . . [but] Moses said to the people, 'Do not be afraid; for God has come only to test you and to put the fear of him upon you so that you do not sin' " (20:18-20). These commandments gave direction, reassurance, and hope to people who had been sure that they were lost and abandoned.

When we read in Psalm 119 the verses that refer to the commandments, we can begin to understand why this ancient people had a feeling about commandments very different from the attitude of many people today. These precepts given to a people God has chosen are first of all a symbol of affection and a sign of commitment. So the psalmist speaks in gratitude as follows:

"See, I have longed for your precepts;
    in your righteousness give me life. . . . (v. 40)
I will keep your law continually,
    forever and ever.
I shall walk at liberty,
    for I have sought your precepts.
I will also speak of your decrees before kings,
    and shall not be put to shame;
I find my delight in your commandments
    because I love them.
I revere your commandments, which I love,
    and I will meditate on your statutes."
                    (vv. 44-48)

Obedience seems hard today largely because it is so misunderstood. But it is not about constraint; the psalmist says that by God's commands, "I shall walk at liberty."

It helps to know that obedience comes from the Latin word *obaudire*, which means to listen with all your heart. The opposite of obedience is not so much disobedience as absurdity (from the Latin *absurdus*, that is, profoundly deaf). Obedience is hearing the voice of the Giver of life and freedom; it is knowing where to seek that voice and learning how to listen from the depths of your heart. But a life totally out of touch with that voice—and its promise and assurance of love and significance—is truly absurd in every sense.

A prevalent but often unacknowledged attitude in the popular culture is that we create ourselves, unencumbered by any debt of veneration or gratitude. This flatters us in good times, but leaves us bereft of comfort in failure and depression. The dominant popular culture seems not to hear the comforting words of God to Moses: "Tell them that I AM has spoken these words to you. . . ." God's commandments are our communication with the fountain of life.

God's commands have a deeper meaning. It is as if God were saying: "All that you do, in everything that you do, do it in the power of my love which gives you life. Make your life and your actions a witness to me: for I have given you life, not death; beauty, not chaos; peace, not turmoil. Hear and obey, and you shall have life. Live in mindfulness of my power and my love."

> *Your word is the law of our life, gracious God:*
> *You speak and we come to be.*
> *Your beloved, Jesus the Christ, is your word to us—*
> *your explanation of love and fullness of life.*
> *Speak to our hearts your design for our being,*
> *speak and we shall obey . . .*
> *shall ourselves become your word in this world.*
> *"Your word is a lamp to my feet*
> *and a light to my path. . . .*

30

Let your hand be ready to help me,
  for I have chosen your precepts.
I long for your salvation, O Lord,
  and your law is my delight.
Let me live that I may praise you,
  and let your ordinances help me.''

                    (Ps 119:105, 173–5)

THE ARK OF THE COVENANT

The campground at Sinai was the place where God indicated to Moses the terms by which the divine presence would remain in the midst of the Exodus pilgrims. The Book of Exodus is filled with details about God's instructions to Moses concerning prophecy and worship. The chief among these concerns the construction of the ark which served as the resting place for the tablets of the Law which God gave to Moses and as the dwelling place of God in the midst of the people.

Chapter 25 of the Book of Exodus describes just how the ark was to be constructed, according to God's own instructions. It was to be a rectangular box fabricated out of acacia wood with rings fastened to the bottom into which carrying poles were fitted, since the ark was to be the journeying chamber within which God accompanied Israel on its exodus travels. It was to have a cover made of wood with the figures of two cherubs (fierce, winged beasts) sculpted in gold at either end facing one another. All these parts were to be enveloped in gold. The cover of the ark was called God's mercy seat: ''There I will meet with you, and from above the mercy seat, from between the two cherubim that are on the ark of the covenant, I will deliver to you all my commands for the Israelites'' (Exod 25:22).

The ark was kept within a tent when it was not being carried on the journey. When finally the Temple was built to house the Lord's dwelling place, the ark was kept behind a veil in a sanctuary where no

33

one but the high priest could enter, and then only once a year, on the Day of Atonement. That place was called the Holy of Holies.

The ark is a powerful sign of both God's presence and God's transcendence. God is closer to our inmost being than we are ourselves; yet God is also unfathomably great—beyond our grasp. The ark represents God's desire to remain close to the people as well as God's incomprehensible holiness. As the reliquary for the tablets of the Law, the ark was both an archive and a treasury. As the mercy seat where God came to converse with Moses, the ark belonged more to God and to heaven than to earth and to the people. In a certain sense, the ark was God's possession, not Israel's: it was made following God's design and it was God's dwelling place in the midst of the people.

As the people of Israel came into the Promised Land, the ark was frequently carried in battle. It was a symbol of God fighting for Israel—a sign of God's presence and power accompanying them in their struggles to take possession of their new homeland. There are details that astound—like God striking down an Israelite named Uzzah who reached out and touched the ark to steady it when it appeared about to fall off the cart that was transporting it. God was angered because Uzzah dared to touch the ark, and struck him dead (2 Sam 6:7). The ark was the visible assurance that the Holy One who made the heavens and the earth and who led Israel forth from slavery in Egypt remained really present in their midst.

This account of the ark of the covenant provides background for contemporary Christian piety. Today many people have been led to stress the aspect of God's presence in the community and to neglect the sacredness of the place where God dwells with special intensity through holy signs. Nonetheless it is important to see that our church buildings are both shrines and meeting houses.

Generations of Catholics (and many Anglican, Orthodox, and Protestants, too) grew up referring to the space where the altar and the tabernacle were placed as the ''sanctuary,'' that is, the holy space. Before the present reform of the liturgy, it would have been rare for the

34

non-ordained to enter the sanctuary except as servers at the altar during sacramental rites.

In the years since Vatican II, Roman Catholics have gained much in emphasizing the actual, present "work" of the Christian assembly in celebrating God's Word and the Eucharist as the bond of community love. Yet some of the dynamics that we have emphasized in order to encourage universal participation, such as using hymns with folksy melodies and impressing inexperienced or untrained people to act as liturgical readers and altar ministers, can have the effect of diminishing the atmosphere of the sacred that the Book of Exodus calls "holiness." The etiquette of sacred rites needs to be imparted to those who generously agree to assist us as ministers in the Church's rites.

The ark of the covenant as a vessel for God's gifts and a privileged site for God's dwelling, of course, reminds Catholics of the role of the tabernacle in our liturgy. Contemporary liturgical legislation leaves no doubt that the purpose of the tabernacle as the place of reservation for the sacrament after Mass is so that the sick, the aged, and others who cannot participate in the Mass can share the Body of Christ. Pastors are encouraged to create Eucharistic chapels apart from the altar and central nave of the church. This is in conformity with the liturgy's clear emphasis upon the priority of the Eucharistic celebration over any other devotional aspect of Eucharistic piety.

But there is still a role for the tabernacle as the symbol of God's dwelling place. While not prescribed as an essential devotion, necessary for every person, personal prayer in private before the tabernacle containing the Eucharistic bread is helpful and sanctifying for many who find there a privileged occasion to converse heart to heart with God in Jesus the Lord. One essential dimension of contemplation is learning to converse with the whole of oneself—learning incarnate prayer where one's senses, muscles, breath, and stillness are the signs of exchange after all our words have come to an end. It is God, after all, who says to us: "Taste and see the goodness of the LORD!" (Ps 34:8).

Like the ark of the covenant for Israel, the tabernacle today invites awe, devotion, and awareness.

You show your holiness to us, O God,
  in ways that stretch our understanding:
You speak in silences, invite us into quiet waiting,
  and manifest your love at the center of our being.
Why do you insist that we enter so deeply
  to see, to hear, to feel your tenderness?
You ask each one of us to be your ark—
  vessel of your word and tabernacle of your presence!
Yet sometimes too we must go apart
  to the place where you dwell—
  where your life is framed in holy signs—
And be replenished with the music of your silence
  and the word of your peace.

THE
GLORY
OF
THE LORD

When I was four years old, my father took my sister and brother and me out into our yard one frosty night to look up into the winter sky. Waves of rose and greenish light flooded across the northern horizon like vast curtains of shimmering satin. I was frightened by the sky's sudden strangeness. The quiet heavens, usually the more serene for countless tiny points of starlight, had become a theater of cosmic energy. But I was also reassured by my father's calmness and by his fascination with a phenomenon that was most unusual for an East-coast December. Ever since, the name *aurora borealis* has had a magic quality for me—for that was what we saw in the winter darkness, the "northern lights."

Now when I pray the opening lines of Psalm 19, I think of the aurora and of other rare crisp evenings when the whole basin of the night was filled with starlight. "The heavens are telling the glory of God; and the firmament proclaims God's handiwork," said the psalmist. The Bible is filled with rich images of God's power that refer to the "glory" or the "presence" of the LORD. The biblical writers want us never to forget that God's actions surpass any words or ideas that we may have to express them.

The strongest expression of God's glory in this sense occurs in the Book of Exodus where the Lord, who appeared to Moses in the burning bush, visibly accompanies the Israelites through the desert to guide their journey. In the words of Exodus: "the LORD went in front of them in a pillar of cloud by day, to lead them along the way, and in a pillar of fire by night, to give them light, so that they might travel by day and night. Neither the pillar of cloud by day nor the pillar of fire by night left its place in front of the people" (Exod 13:21-22).

The Lord's glory is the sign of power and authority. God arranged with Moses to appear when necessary at the entrance to the meeting tent that housed the tablets of the commandments: "At the entrance of the tent of meeting, I will meet with you, to speak to you there. I will meet with the Israelites there, and it shall be sanctified by my glory" (Exod 29:42-43). Repeatedly the Lord calmed and persuaded—indeed intimidated—the Israelites by the manifestation of divine glory. On Mount Sinai, the tablets of the Law were handed to Moses to the accompaniment of God's great Amen: "When all the people witnessed the thunder and lightning, the sound of the trumpet, and the mountain smoking, they were afraid and trembled and stood at a distance, and said to Moses: 'You speak to us, and we will listen; but do not let God speak to us, or we will die'" (Exod 20:18-19).

The tradition of the Jews is instructive. *Yahweh*, the holy name that God revealed to Moses, was thought after their return from the Exile too sacred to be pronounced. Though they wrote the consonants of this holy name in the scroll of their Scriptures, they did not pronounce it when they read aloud. They used instead the Hebrew word *Adonai*, "my LORD," out of respect for God's holiness. The Jews found it unimaginable that someone could meet the living God and not be consumed by divine energy. The exceptional case of Moses is a perfect illustration.

"Moses said to the LORD, 'Show me your glory, I pray.' And the LORD said, 'I will make all my goodness pass before you, and will proclaim before you the name, YHWH (the LORD); and I will be gracious to whom I will be gracious. But you cannot see my face; for no one shall see me and live.' And the LORD continued, 'See, there is a place by me where you shall stand on the rock; and while my glory passes by I will put you in a cleft of the rock, and I will cover you with

40

my hand until I have passed by; then I will take away my hand, and you shall see my back; but my face shall not be seen'" (Exod 33:18-23). This is a sign of the great intimacy that the prophet had with God. No wonder that this people prayed: "Tremble, O earth, at the presence of the LORD, at the presence of the God of Jacob" (Ps 114:7).

When another prophet, Isaiah, received his call, the glory of God filled the temple as a witness to God's presence and authority. "In the year that King Uzziah died, I saw the LORD sitting on a throne, high and lofty; and the hem of his robe filled the temple. Seraphs were in attendance above him; each had six wings: with two they covered their faces, and with two they covered their feet, and with two they flew. And one called to another and said: 'Holy, holy, holy is the LORD of hosts; the whole earth is full of his glory.' The pivots on the thresholds shook at the voices of those who called, and the house filled with smoke" (Isa 6:1-5).

This prophet's vision, filled with strange imagery, provides us with a sublime expression of awe and submission that has become one of the core ritual expressions of Christian believers. The words of the seraphs are included in the rite of the Mass as the song of acclamation before God's action in the Eucharistic Prayer. When we pray "Holy, holy, holy, Lord; God of power and might," we take to ourselves Isaiah's dispositions of reverence and obedience. We are in the presence of the glory of the Lord.

Isaiah sensed the trouble he was in: "Woe is me! I am lost, for I am a man of unclean lips" (6:5). But one of the seraphs flew over to him with a burning altar coal held by a pair of tongs. With it the seraph touched the mouth of Isaiah and said: "Now that this has touched your lips, your guilt has departed and your sin is blotted out" (6:7). Then the prophet heard God's voice: "Whom shall I send?" and he responded: "Here I am; send me!" (6:8). This reverie of the prophet is evocative of dream symbols. Isaiah is powerless before the overabundance of his feelings about God's majesty and his own worthlessness. At the same time he is utterly convinced of the reality of God's action in his life.

When we take this imagery over into our sacred rituals we identify with the attitude and spirit of the prophet. Like Moses and Isaiah, even though we have been called by God into relation and intimacy, we still cannot fathom the mystery that speaks to our hearts. God is God—beyond our comprehension. Yet we have to acknowledge that God's presence transforms and purifies our lives.

Thomas Aquinas pondered this mystery and came up with a strange solution. The name for God, he thought, is not a noun but a verb: in Latin he called God not *ens* (Being), but *esse* (to Be).[8] God is not a static reality on a cosmic shelf. God is active everywhere in the sense that wherever anything exists, God's is the present, active force of its existence. There is no escaping this God. As Thomas saw it, wherever we express life, we participate in the energy of God's life made present in us.

If this is true, how could we miss seeing or believing in God? Some philosophers like to say that detecting the difference between something that is always and everywhere present and something that is nowhere and never present is next to impossible. This might be true except for that fact that God, always and everywhere present, calls out to us to recognize the glory of the divine presence—and usually overwhelms us in such a moment of truth. It is also likely that when we meet the living God, we will do so only in the cleft of a rock, the quiet of the temple, or the still movement of a light breeze (1 Kgs 19:12). God hides the plenitude of divine reality to teach us new habits of subtlety. This is how we learn to attend to the presence of our hidden God.

When Christians assemble at prayer, they frequently invoke the divine and ask for the grace to know God's presence. Each morning, at the beginning of their liturgies of praise, monastic communities pray: "Come, let us sing to the LORD; let us come into his presence with thanksgiving. Come, let us worship and bow down, let us kneel before the LORD, our Maker" (Ps 95:1-2, 6). Applying this same instinct to the prayer of all God's people, the liturgy constitution of Vatican II taught as follows: "We sing a hymn to the Lord's glory with all the warriors of the heavenly army; venerating the memory of the saints, we hope for some part and fellowship with them; we eagerly await the Savior, our Lord Jesus Christ, until He, our life, shall appear and we too will appear with Him in glory."[9]

> *Holy God, Holy Strong One, Holy Deathless One,*
> > *have mercy on us.*
> *You are glorified by the ranks of holy beings in the eternal kingdom,*
> > *you are adored by all your redeemed and chosen ones.*
> *You brought all things from nothing into being,*
> > *you made human creatures in your own likeness.*
> *You give us the power to stand before your glory*
> > *and to acknowledge your beauty and your love,*
> > *even as we acknowledge that we know not who you really are.*
> *You are holy, you are life, you are mercy:*
> > *we give glory to you.*

ALTARS

Through the whole story of God's people, the making of altars is a key feature of communication between heaven and earth. Chapter 12 of the Book of Genesis tells with great simplicity the story of Abram being called from his town of Haran to go at God's insistence to the land of Canaan. With Sarai his wife and Lot his nephew, Abram brought all his belongings to this new country to settle down. "Then the LORD appeared to Abram, and said, 'To your offspring I will give this land.' So he built there an altar to the LORD, who had appeared to him" (Gen 12:7). As elsewhere in the Old Testament, the building of an altar is a symbol of God's visitation, a testimony to people's experience of receiving a call or a message, and a reminder of God's promises and God's nearness. Building an altar is a way of saying "Amen" to the awesome fact that God has entered our lives.

An altar is the place where our profound human aspirations to interact with God are reciprocated by God's action in our midst. Abraham (formerly called Abram) accepts the role of building up a people to be God's special possession; he responds to God with reverence and obedience. Then Abraham hears God calling him to offer in sacrifice the dearest possession in his life, his own son Isaac—an unimaginable test of faith which evokes for Christian believers God's sacrifice of his own son, Jesus, for our salvation. Obeying up to the very moment of completing the sacrifice of Isaac, Abraham at the last instant hears his name called again by the angel of the Lord: " 'Abraham!: Do not lay

45

your hand on the boy; for now I know that you fear God. . . .' And Abraham looked up and saw a ram, caught in a thicket by its horns. Abraham went and took the ram and offered it up as a burnt offering instead of his son'' (Gen 22:11-13). God attends to our hearts and our actions as we approach the altar that is our meeting place.

An altar is weighted with far-reaching significance. It is a raised-up place, established between earth and heaven: the surface of the altar says by its design that it is a place for the meeting between all that dwells below and all that reigns on high. It is the symbolic midpoint between heaven and earth; just creating such a place is an act of faith and a sign of devotion.

Biblical altars were built of heavy stones as if to say, ''Here is where God may be met—here is the place.'' Symbolically an altar is the axis of the world around which all reality revolves. In placing a sacrifice or a gift upon the altar, I bring from the context of my life something precious and representative of myself and set it before the Holy One who has entered this space before and will enter it again. To eat a meal sacrificed upon such an altar is to break bread and share sacred nourishment with God: God offers us hospitality in the very space which we have created to celebrate God's coming into our lives.

Altars are signs of human solidarity as well. In Exodus, after receiving the commandments of God on the mount of Sinai, Moses ''rose early in the morning, and built an altar at the foot of the mountain, and set up twelve pillars, corresponding to the twelve tribes of Israel'' (Exod 24:4). This altar is not only a symbol of the place where God comes to meet us, it is also a symbol of our unity of spirit as people bound together by our common reverence for the Lord. When the Israelites finally cross into the Promised Land, Joshua makes a memorial of the event: ''Joshua set up twelve stones in the middle of the Jordan, in the place where the priests bearing the ark of the covenant had stood; and they are there to this day'' (Josh 4:9). The exodus people— the tribes of Israel—left their markers behind in those places where God had saved them and opened up history before them. Something of ourselves should go into the construction of the altar.

It is fascinating that the Jewish people, who received the commandment against idolatry (Deut 5:8-10) and honored it with such unflinching zeal, remained so attached to the imagery of the altar. Unlike a statue or a painting, an altar is not a representation in graphic form of some other thing, but a marker of a place and an event: the place where God may be met and the event of God's touching our inmost spirit. In our places of prayer, our altars are meant to be noble, worthy signs of this reality. It is unfortunate that the power of this symbolism is frequently lost. We forget the biblical tradition or try to accommodate the altar to its homey aspect as a banquet or Communion table.

It is inappropriate for an altar to be used like just any table—a place where papers and books are left lying around, a convenient place to put a vase or pot of flowers or to tack a banner for the decoration of the room. There should be an immense dignity to the altar even apart from its utilitarian moments of serving for the Eucharistic meal. It should never be used as a table or shelf for anything but the Eucharistic sacrifice.

The concept of the altar challenges us to maintain reverence and a feeling of transcendence in our worship and our prayer. Blessed are those who can enter a holy space and find in the altar's symbolic form a sign of the continuing conversation—conducted without benefit of words—between the awesome presence of God and the vast hunger of the human heart.

> *As we gaze upon the altar, the place where people gather*
> *who are called to be Christ's body,*
> *We recognize a different geography than the one we find*
> *worked out on maps and road signs.*
> *For here is the place where Isaac was offered, where Jacob rested*
> *on his journey, where Elijah staked his life on God's*
> *attentive support of him as prophet;*
> *Here too are the hidden, mysterious places where our ancestors*
> *sensed the power and the presence of God and built their*
> *tables of thanksgiving and adoration;*

Here is Golgotha—the rock upon which the altar of the crucified
was lifted up for us.
Speak for us, pillar of rock where earth meets heaven, table of
sacrifice, memorial monument of divine encounters:
Say for our eyes and our hearts what our words have no power
to utter: that we are here and you are here, Holy One,
and that our waiting is love and trust in your promise.

MYSTERIES

I want their hearts to be encouraged and united in love,
     so that they may have . . .
     the knowledge of God's mystery, that is, Christ himself.

Colossians 2:2

MOTHER
OF
GOD

"O chosen one—full of grace,
all creation, the hosts of angels, and the human race rejoice in you:
holy sanctuary, spiritual paradise, glory of virgins
from whom God took flesh,
he who was God before all time became a little child within you.
Your lap was his throne; your womb he made greater than the sky.
All creatures are joyful because of you: you are full of grace."
                              (Byzantine Liturgy of Saint Basil)[10]

Human beings are drawn naturally toward their mothers as to the
source of their life. Psychologists assure us that newborn infants are
nurtured in their rock-bottom intuition of the trustworthiness of life
and of the world by the secret dialogue of glances and smiles that they
exchange with their mothers in their earliest months. This contemplative activity of infants, communicating complete trust in their mothers
through mute affection and mirroring smiles, lays the foundation for
the affective dialogues of the rest of their lives. Infants' experiences of
mother love are their first clues to the immensity of life. Our mothers
provide our first images of God.

   For centuries, the privileged image of Mary in the Western
Church showed her seated with her Son, the Word of God, resting in
her lap. This style of imagery was derived from the practice of the
Eastern Church. Mary holds the child facing out toward those who approach. Her gesture represents her role as *Theotokos*, the Greek word

used by the fourth-century Church to describe Mary as "God-bearer." By her own trusting assent to God's invitation for her to become the mother of "the Son of the Most High" (Luke 1:32), her entire life took on universal meaning. She became forever the maternal link between God and humanity, giving human nature to the eternal one from her own flesh and blood. Her words at the annunciation are a model for us of openness in faith: "Here I am, the servant of the LORD; let it be with me according to your word" (1:38).

This maternal image of Mary also shows her to be the nurturer and strengthener of the child Jesus. We discover God like to us in human flesh by looking into the arms of her whom we call "Mother of God." The relation of this mother and son is filled with all the dynamics of undoubted love and faithful nurturing that mark successful mothering in any life. Mary is both the parent of a human child "born of a woman" (Gal 4:4) and also the "lowly servant" (Luke 1:48) of God. She acknowledges her cooperation: "the Mighty One has done great things to me" (Luke 1:49). She represents both our creatureliness and the perfect obedience of the servant of God. She is more aware than anyone else of human inadequacy in the presence of God's immensity. Yet she knows a greater intimacy with God than any other creature.

In the image before us, her son is symbolized by an open book with the letters *IHC* and *XP* drawn to represent the Greek words *Jesus* and *Christ*—names that mean "savior" and "anointed one." In this fashion the drawing conveys the profound mystery of Mary's role in our redemption. Every aspect of human maternity entered into the unique phenomenon of divine incarnation by reason of Mary's free cooperation with God's call to her to be Christ's mother. It is fitting to picture her as the throne of God's word to the world.

Mary herself is the model of the contemplative life. She is the exemplary listener who was able to obey God's unimaginable invitation to become the bearer of God's own child. As noted before, the word *obedience* comes from ancient roots in Greek and Latin that mean "intense listening." Mary's obedience arises from her total attention to

52

the subtle action of God in her life. Her will is thus shaped to conform to God's plan.

The central mystery of Mary's life is her freedom. God asks her to give her life for the divine plan of salvation. Her obedience is so profound that it in no way diminishes her autonomy. ''Blessed is she who believed that there would be a fulfillment of what was spoken to her by the Lord'' (Luke 1:45). Mary's spontaneity of response and depth of self-giving create a new moment in human history. ''Surely, from now on all generations will call me blessed'' (Luke 1:48).

Luke's Gospel narrates a wonderful moment during Jesus' preaching: ''a woman in the crowd raised her voice and said to him, 'Blessed is the womb that bore you and the breasts that nursed you!' But he said, 'Blessed rather are those who hear the word of God and obey it!' '' (11:27). Mary's obedience, which Jesus praised in this mysterious word, included her continuing participation in the preaching and ministry of her son. Simeon had prophesied of her: ''a sword will pierce your own soul too'' (Luke 2:35). She had to carry deep within her heart all the vulnerability, wounds, and sacrifice that fell upon her child.

Looking upon the image of the mother who is the throne of the eternal word, we can find both delight and power in the following words which the eighth-century Greek Akathist Hymn places on the lips of the archangel Gabriel:

''Hail, Partaker of the ineffable secret;
    hail, Believer in the holy plan that must be held in silence.
Hail, Inaugurator of the marvels of the Christ;
    hail, Consummation of all the teachings that explain him.
Hail, heavenly Ladder on which God descended among us;
    hail, Bridge binding together earth and heaven.
Hail, Marvel who fascinates the angels;
    hail, endless Desolation of the demons.
Hail, inexpressible Bearer of eternal Light;
    hail, you who have never betrayed the mystery of your fruitfulness.

Hail, Wisdom beyond the science of the sages;
   hail, Enlightenment of the spirits of believers.
Greetings, undiminished Spouse of God!"[11]

Holy God, help us to find in the mother of your Son
   an example of fullness of life;
as she was attentive to your will and responded with love,
   so may we also find peace in obedience to your word.
Through her prayers for us, give rest to the weary,
   comfort to those who mourn, pardon to sinners,
   and grace and salvation to all people.
Like Mary, may we treasure Christ her son in our hearts
   and carry him to everyone we meet.

THE LAMB OF GOD

John the Baptist, preaching and baptizing in Bethany beyond the Jordan, looked up and said to his disciples: "Here is the Lamb of God who takes away the sin of the world!" (John 1:29). John, the prophet, was aware that his mission differed greatly from that of the one whose coming he prepared for by his rites of repentance. This "Lamb of God" would be the sacrificial offering whose gift of his life would complete all the ritual sacrifices of the old covenant and bring into being a new covenant with God. This Lamb lived in the midst of those he saved and transformed their lives by loving them with perfect love.

The image of the lamb appears throughout the Bible. It is a symbol at once natural and mysterious. For farmers who raised sheep, the lamb is the appropriate and natural offering of something both dear to them and representative of their lives. A yearling lamb is an ideal image of innocence, appealing beauty, spontaneous freshness, animal playfulness, and perfect docility. Jeremiah uses this image of simplicity to express his openness to the destiny which God worked in his life: "But I was like a gentle lamb led to the slaughter" (11:19).

The prophet Isaiah also develops this imagery. The prophet's picture of the Servant of God compares his patience and mute endurance to that of the lamb:

"He was oppressed, and he was afflicted,
    yet he did not open his mouth;

like a lamb that is led to the slaughter,
    and like a sheep that before its shearers is silent,
    so he did not open his mouth. . . .
Yet it was the will of the LORD to crush him with pain.
When you make his life an offering for sin,
    he shall see his offspring, and shall prolong his days;
through him the will of the LORD shall prosper.
Out of his anguish he shall see light.''

(Isa 53:7, 10-11)

The prophets of course were well aware of the deeply symbolic meaning of the lamb as the principal food of the paschal meal. Moses instructed the elders of Israel to prepare for their deliverance from slavery by cooking a special feast to ready them for their departure: ''Go, select lambs for your families, and slaughter the passover lamb. Take a bunch of hyssop, dip it in the blood that is in the basin, and touch the lintel and the two doorposts with the blood in the basin. . . . When he sees the blood on the lintel and on the two doorposts, the LORD will pass over that door and will not allow the destroyer to enter your houses to strike you down'' (Exod 12:21-22, 23).

The blood of the lamb marks the doorways of the Israelites so that the avenging angel who will slaughter the first-born of the Egyptians will pass by or ''pass over.'' But this symbolism takes on new dimensions in the Book of Revelation, where those who have entered into the chorus of eternal thanksgiving are described as follows: ''These are they who have come out of the great ordeal; they have washed their robes and made them white in the blood of the Lamb. . . . [T]he Lamb at the center of the throne will be their shepherd, and he will guide them to springs of the water of life, and God will wipe away every tear from their eyes'' (7:14, 17).

This imagery is unfathomable. The Lamb is also the Shepherd. Jesus told the apostles: ''I am the good shepherd. The good shepherd lays down his life for the sheep'' (John 10:11). In Matthew, Jesus says: ''If a shepherd has a hundred sheep, and one of them has gone astray,

58

does he not leave the ninety-nine on the mountains and go in search of the one that went astray?'' (18:12). This good shepherd gives his life for their safety. The Good Shepherd and the Paschal Lamb are one.

The Epistle of Peter adds this: ''You know that you were ransomed from the futile ways inherited from your ancestors, not with perishable things like silver or gold, but with the precious blood of Christ, like that of a lamb without defect or blemish'' (1 Pet 1:18-19). The epistle's words are telling for our age. We are ransomed not just from sin, guilt, and punishment; we are ransomed from ''futility''— from meaninglessness. In a world overloaded with pleasures, frequently the one thing lacking is meaningful direction.

The direction offered by the Lamb of God embraces the whole of our energies—as 1 Peter explains: ''Come to him, a living stone, though rejected by mortals yet precious and chosen in God's sight, and like living stones, let yourselves be built into a spiritual house, to be a holy priesthood, to offer spiritual sacrifices acceptable to God through Jesus Christ'' (2:4-5). Our lives can be bound together into a community that is like a holy building, built upon the cornerstone that is the Christ. This gift of community, mutual service in love and respect, gives human life its quality. Everything that such a community does is precious in the eyes of God.

Finally the Lamb who is the Shepherd (see Rev 7:17) leads us on toward a feast that belongs more properly to the heavenly Jerusalem than to the earthly Church. While here among us, Christ did everything possible to endow our lives with meaning. He attacked injustice, healed illness, spread the good news of a transformed world, up to the moment that he was obliged to give his life to gain eternal life for us. He calls us to continue the same kind of compassionate care for this world that he modelled for us: ''Love one another as I have loved you'' (John 15:12). But he lets us know that ''here we have no lasting city, but we are looking for the city that is to come'' (Heb 13:14).

John of Patmos, the author of Revelation, tells us how this city that is to come appeared to him: ''I saw no temple in the city, for its temple is the LORD God the Almighty and the Lamb. And the city has no need of sun or moon to shine on it, for the glory of God is its light, and its lamp is the Lamb" (21:22-23). Even now we are drawn toward that heavenly light, for there is our Shepherd who knows us by name and who wills that none of us be lost.

Lamb of God, favored and chosen by the Author of life,
    you became for our sake a sacrament of trust and obedience
    to mold our lives into fitting vessels for God's grace and power.
Though renouncing violence, you were its victim;
    though innocent, you became one with our burden of sin.
We name you Lamb of God at the moment
    that we receive you in the Bread of Life.
Be our bread of readiness:
    sustain us as we flee from familiar slavery
    and journey across desert paths toward true freedom.
You take away the sin of the world:
    have mercy on us.

THE TRANSFIGURA-TION OF JESUS

Between sending out the Twelve with "power and authority over all demons and to cure diseases" in order to proclaim the kingdom of God (Luke 9:2) and his final entry into Jerusalem, Jesus took Peter, John, and James up onto a mountain to pray. This was a moment of spiritual and psychological transformation for all of them.

In the gospel accounts Jesus became incandescent; his clothes became charged with brightness. The prophets Moses and Elijah became visible to the apostles, and the prophets "appeared in glory and were speaking of his departure, which he was about to accomplish in Jerusalem" (Luke 9:31). As they watched, a cloud came and enveloped the scene, and from the cloud the apostles heard a voice saying, "This is my Son, my Chosen; listen to him!" (Luke 9:35).

The transfiguration of Jesus depicts a decisive moment in Jesus' life, when God's compassionate love enters into his being with such intensity that he becomes luminous with the energy of divine power. Jesus becomes transparent to the light of the One who sends him into the world. The completeness of Jesus' obedience to God's voice claims his entire being. God's radiance becomes manifest in his flesh.

In Jesus' prayer on the mountain with his closest friends, he makes the whole of his person open, supple, ready for the word of the Father. Jesus becomes the sacrament of prayer: he shows us the splendor of God dwelling in and transforming a bodily person into an icon of God's presence. The luminosity of God's dwelling in the flesh of Jesus tells us that God desires to transform all human flesh. By the mystery of his transfiguration, Jesus gives us the grace to accept God's plan to divinize flesh—to convert us into true children of God.

This prayer of Jesus on the mountain is like the prayer that he will soon come to in the garden of Gethsemani. It is a prayer of struggle to understand, to remain open to the plan of God, and to accept the dreadful passion that will change human destiny. In the garden Jesus will pray, ''Father, if you are willing, remove this cup from me; yet, not my will but yours be done'' (Luke 22:42). In the garden also the intensity of Jesus' prayer envelops his whole being; but that moment is different: it is already the inauguration of his passion. ''In his anguish he prayed more earnestly, and his sweat became like great drops of blood falling down on the ground'' (Luke 22:44). In the garden, as at the transfiguration, he receives comfort from God's holy beings: ''an angel from heaven appeared to him and gave him strength'' (Luke 22:43). Jesus is not left alone in Gethsemani or on the mount of transfiguration.

Did Moses remind Jesus of his own mountain prayer before the burning bush, when he asked God to select another to be Israel's liberator? Did he repeat God's words to him: ''I have observed the misery of my people who are in Egypt; I have heard their cry . . . I have come down to deliver them . . .'' (Exod 3:7-8)? Did Elijah share with Jesus his moment of desolation when, wearied from his preaching to a nation sunk in idolatry, he told God on the mountain: ''I have been very zealous for the LORD, the God of hosts; for the Israelites have forsaken your covenant, thrown down your altars, and killed your prophets with the sword. I alone am left, and they are seeking my life, to take it away'' (1 Kgs 19:10)?

The prophets who meet with Jesus on the mount of transfiguration help him humanly to understand that he is about to fulfill the work of liberation that was prefigured in Moses and the Exodus, that he is about to live out the same vulnerability unto death that Elijah so feared. This encounter also brought Jesus to understand definitively

64

that he is himself the vessel of Godhead, he is the Beloved, he is the eternal Lord God in flesh for the sake of the world. Jesus' prayer is his ''Amen'' to his Father's will: he is about to bring the work of the prophets to its consummation.

For us, Jesus' transfiguration can be a great comfort. We observe the apostles struggling to understand their friend Jesus. In this secret and transforming moment, they receive a glimpse of the fullness of Jesus' holiness and the power of his redeeming work. St. John Damascene's words are apt: Jesus ''was transfigured, not by acquiring what he was not but by manifesting to his disciples what he in fact was; he opened their eyes and gave these blind men sight.''[12] The apostles too are transfigured to the degree that their eyes are given new power to see and their hearts new power to believe.

Perhaps our transfiguration moment will come when we realize that God is not an idea, but the ground of our existence. Perhaps we will be transfigured when we recognize that we are sustained in existence by a present mercy of divine love. Perhaps we will be re-made into apostles when we recognize that Jesus came to show us the profound meaning that emptiness, suffering, and bottomless yearning can have when we live it with faith in God's love for us.

Our transfiguration has everything to do with our personal, committed relationship to Jesus Christ. This relationship does not spare us pain, but it does unite us with transforming love in the midst of pain. Jesus' love is a personal act of commitment to me as a unique individual. In response I give myself to the plan that Jesus preached; I become a witness to God's kingdom. With human language, we can speak only abstractly about what we experience concretely.

We speak about God, but what we know is immeasurable love. We speak about grace, but what we know is being forgiven. We speak about obedience, but what we know is the joy that comes from gratefully returning a favor to a divine Friend. Or we *don't* know this, perhaps. But such knowing is transfiguration. As we gaze on the image of the transfiguration of Jesus, we can hope for this conversion of understanding and feeling and energy. We can look for the light.

Jesus, you prepared for your death
    not as the end of your work, but as its fulfillment.
You entered into dialogue with your beloved Father
    remembering the work of Moses and Elijah:
you hungered for liberation and illumination for your people
    even as you opened your heart in dread to the shadow of death.
Your transfiguration is reassurance for our fragile faith,
    an instrument to transform our prayer.
Help us to be unafraid of hidden mountain retreats,
    of the unexplained questions of our lives,
    and of our mute search to understand your Father's will.
Make us brave by teaching us compassion;
    transform us in prayer to carry your work of liberation
    to the ends of our lives—and to the ends of the earth.

THE CRUCIFIX-ION

Jesus is lifted up on the tree of the cross. He has finished his mission of preaching the kingdom of God and healing those who came to him in faith, giving new life to the sick, the crippled, the blind, the deaf, the mute, and the outcast. Matthew's Gospel, in awe of Jesus' miracles, says that Jesus fulfilled "what had been spoken through the prophet Isaiah, 'He took our infirmities and bore our diseases'" (8:17). The suffering servant of the Lord here brings his ministry to the climax that was foreshadowed in the prophecy of Isaiah:

> "Surely he has borne our infirmities
>   and carried our diseases;
> yet we accounted him stricken,
>   struck down by God, and afflicted.
> But he was wounded for our transgressions,
>   crushed for our iniquities;
> upon him was the punishment that made us whole,
>   and by his bruises we are healed. . . .
> He poured himself out to death,
>   and was numbered with the transgressors;
> yet he bore the sins of many,
>   and made intercession for the transgressors."
> (Isa 53:4-5, 12)

In the vision of this biblical word, we earthly pilgrims are burdened with a combination of physical vulnerability, moral frailty, sin, and the prospect of death. This describes our predicament as creatures who have inherited a world whose integrity is damaged by sin and sundered from its proper relation with its creator. We have no clear idea what to make of our situation.

Into this milieu comes Jesus of Nazareth, the charismatic preacher who revealed himself to be God's definitive prophet—God's own child. He shocked people by proclaiming God's mercy and forgiveness directly to all persons, regardless of race, class, tribe, or religion. He convinced many that he was from God by exercising divine power to change lost lives through healing and miracles. This is the Jesus who entered into the final drama of God's manifestation of redemptive love when he was nailed to the cross.

St. Paul succinctly summarizes the consequences of this drama of the crucifixion in these cryptic phrases:

—"For our sake [God] made him to be sin who knew no sin, so that in him we might become the righteousness of God"(2 Cor 5:21).

—"Jesus . . . was handed over to death for our trespasses and was raised for our justification" (Rom 4:25).

—"Christ redeemed us from the curse of the law by becoming a curse for us . . ." (Gal 3:13).

All our vague dread of our vulnerability, our fear of dying, our gnawing sense of our moral frailties, and our clear consciousness of our particular acts of injustice, cruelty, and pettiness—all this becomes integrated into the mystery described by Paul. We are saved.

The cross of Christ has taken up our mortality and our weakness. If we have faith in the one lifted up, we will find life, not death, beyond the pains and tragedy of the cross. Through this mystery of dying for us, Christ entered into life. "Although he was [God's] son, he learned obedience through what he suffered; and having been made perfect, he became the source of eternal salvation for all who obey him . . ." (Heb 5:8-9).

Roman Catholic, Orthodox, and some Protestant Christians spend a lifetime marking themselves with the sign of the cross. With their right hand, they trace the trajectory of the vertical and the horizontal branches of Christ's instrument of execution over the front of their body—a sign of blessing and an invocation of the power of Christ's mystery of transformation. For the cross of Christ is the Passover of the New Testament: it is our flight from sin into grace, from slavery into freedom, and from certain death into a journey toward new life. That Passover grace, won on the cross, enters into our anxious hearts, our endurance of pain and illness, our struggles for justice, and our efforts at sacrificial love. The mystery of the cross is not about satisfying the revenge of an angry God; it is a lesson about God's most radical decision to share divine life with us.

"[Christ Jesus,] though he was in the form of God, did not regard equality with God as something to be exploited, but emptied himself, taking the form of a slave, being born in human likeness. And being found in human form, he humbled himself and became obedient to the point of death—even death on a cross" (Phil 2:6-8). Paul continues to explain that our Savior, the Christ, "will transform the body of our humiliation that it may be conformed to the body of his glory, by the power that also enables him to make all things subject to himself" (3:21). The Son of God has entered into our human world to bring us the divine life that is our destiny through faith. As another witness puts it, "We know love by this, that he laid down his life for us—and we ought to lay down our lives for one another" (1 John 3:16).

The words of Jesus, "I have a baptism with which to be baptized, and what stress I am under until it is completed!" (Luke 12:50) refer to his cross. These words show us the sense in which we enter into the mystery of Christ's redemptive action through that baptism which is our own suffering life, lived in hope of God's deliverance. God shows us in Jesus' fidelity to his Father's will what authentic human integrity looks like.

Although we often live our days in denial of our mortality, the Church confronts us daily with the message that we are mortal and that we are saved. "Dying, you destroyed our death; rising you restored our life: Lord Jesus, come in glory!" Each day the Church prays this, affirming the mystery that God entered fully into our human predicament and transformed it, conquering the power of death by the obedience of Jesus upon the cross. That cross is both the sign of death's power and the instrument of our immortality. "If we have died with him, we will also live with him" are words that Paul calls "a sure saying" (2 Tim 2:11). Our life too is a paschal mystery—a mystery of transformation where we learn to live with hope in the face of suffering, struggles, and death.

Vatican II's constitution on the Church uses this imagery to summarize the life of the Church in this world: "The Church, like a pilgrim in a foreign land, presses forward amid the persecutions of the world and the consolations of God, announcing the cross and death of the Lord until He comes (cf. 1 Cor 11:26). By the power of the risen Lord, she is given strength to overcome patiently and lovingly the afflictions and hardships which assail her from within and without, and to show forth to the world the mystery of the Lord in a faithful though shadowed way, until at the last it will be revealed in total splendor."[13]

Each day has its share of dying,
*   each plan has its unmet potential;*
each heart has its pain and sadness
*   linked by love to the grief of others.*
Christ lifted up, you are the sign of the great mystery
*   that God gives life in death, freedom through suffering,*
*   hope in the face of annihilation, and peace in the gift of love.*
Let us enter our pain with you, unafraid of dying
*   the little daily dying*
*   and the transforming paschal dying*
*   when, one with you in faith, we leave this pilgrimage*
*   and enter your kingdom of eternal love.*
You who were broken and who died for us
*   give us now your new life beyond fear,*
*   beyond death.*

THE
EMPTY
TOMB

The empty tomb is an elusive symbol. It bears witness that Jesus, who has died, is no longer held captive by death. But it throws us immediately into the realm of faith, where our trust in the Lord's promises and our sensitivity to his presence in our lives provide the hidden persuasion that makes Christian life possible.

The Gospel according to Mark offers this account: ''When the sabbath was over, Mary Magdalene, and Mary the mother of James, and Salome brought spices so that they might go and anoint him. . . . As they entered the tomb, they saw a young man, dressed in a white robe, sitting on the right side; and they were alarmed. But he said to them, 'Do not be alarmed; you are looking for Jesus of Nazareth, who was crucified. He has been raised; he is not here. Look, there is the place they laid him' '' (Mark 16:1, 5-6). Matthew's Gospel calls the young man an angel; there the angel speaks to them to say, ''Come and see the place where he lay'' (28:6).

The story of the empty tomb is the story of the dawning awareness in the lives of Jesus' friends that all along he had been preparing them for something that they could not grasp. Now that he has crossed the frontier beyond ordinary social communion into a new life, the disciples slowly awaken to the realization that they must reorient themselves to a new life of the Spirit. Paul summarized things this way: ''We have been buried with [Christ] in baptism into death, so that, just as Christ was raised from the dead by the glory of the Father, so we too might walk in newness of life'' (Rom 6:4).

It is probably correct to say that the mystery of the resurrection of Jesus simply cannot be communicated to anyone who remains apart from the life of the redeemed community. The resurrection is not intelligible as an abstract idea; indeed, in 1 Corinthians Paul says that ''the message about the cross is foolishness to those who are perishing, but to us who are being saved it is the power of God'' (1:18). Just as Jesus' resurrection is not his resuscitation to return to the kind of life he had before, so also our resurrection faith does not center on the physical fact so much as on new moral and spiritual possibilities for our lives as we enter a world transformed by Christ's victory over death.

From the earliest preaching of the gospel, believers were vividly aware that under any aspect other than a call in faith, the cross and resurrection of Jesus were not only difficult to understand, but an affront to normal human expectations. In the gospel narratives, those who come to learn of Jesus' resurrection mystery are commissioned immediately to enter into the project of proclamation: ''Go, tell his disciples and Peter that he is going ahead of you to Galilee; there you will see him, just as he told you'' (Mark 16:7). The Scriptures proceed, especially in Luke and John, to describe the appearances of Jesus to those who had committed their lives to him; they describe how he prepared and empowered them for ''the sacred and imperishable proclamation of eternal salvation'' (Mark 16:8 [shorter ending]).

The empty tomb is a powerful symbol of metamorphosis, a crucible of transformation where the human paradox of faith in the unseen and of trust in the physically absent becomes fruitful. Because of the mystery of Christ's burial and being raised, we who believe can find at the tomb joy in sorrow, life in death, light in darkness, freedom in captivity, and hope in fear. There is no greater insult to the dignity of living flesh than the tomb. There is no more powerful message about the ultimate meaning of life than resurrection.

For the disciples the pain of Jesus' death is the pain of loss. As we do when we lose our loved ones, they had to establish a new spiritual geography that reached beyond Jesus' physical absence in order to be united with the Lord. However, in their resurrection faith they recognized that Jesus had tried to anticipate their crisis before his death. In the supper discourse of John's Gospel, Jesus tells them, ''A little while, and you will no longer see me, and again a little while and you will see me . . . you will weep and mourn, but the world will rejoice; you will have pain, but your pain will turn into joy . . . I will see you again, and your hearts will rejoice, and no one will take your joy from you'' (John 16:19-22). Their sorrow becomes transmuted into joy.

In John's Gospel, Jesus teaches the disciples about his identity and his mission in these words: ''I am the light of the world. Whoever follows me will never walk in darkness but will have the light of life'' (8:12). This saying takes place in a dialogue with the Pharisees who are portrayed as partisans of a blind legalism that cannot respond to Jesus' offer of new light and life. John's Gospel is written with a strong contrast between the symbolic force of light and a world of darkness: ''The light shines in the darkness, and the darkness did not overcome it'' (1:5).

Jesus' cross is his struggle with the powers of darkness; his resurrection is the triumph of new life appearing as the light of the world. Second Corinthians extends this imagery to its impact upon our moral and psychological life: ''For it is the God who said, 'Let light shine out of darkness,' who has shone in our hearts to give the light of the knowledge of the glory of God in the face of Jesus Christ'' (v. 6). From the dark tomb emerges the light of God, recalling the lines of Psalm 139: ''the darkness is not dark to you; the night is as bright as the day, for darkness is as light to you'' (v. 12). The tomb may be the end of the road for those who have not believed in Jesus' message: ''I came that they may have life, and have it abundantly'' (John 10:10). But in the grace of the resurrection, this symbol of terminal emptiness becomes the source of ultimate renewal.

Hidden in the shadow of Jesus' tomb is the true lesson of the resurrection. By Paul's account, Jesus came to transform our world into a new creation by preparing us for the gift of the Holy Spirit and promising us a life of communion with God. ''If the Spirit of [the One] who raised Jesus from the dead dwells in you, he who raised Jesus from the dead will give life to your mortal bodies also through the Spirit that dwells in you'' (Rom 8:11).

This same Spirit that is God's power of new life for those who believe in Jesus is able to transform the reality we live in. But God's plan is for the Spirit to transform creation through the cooperation of believers. ''For the creation waits with eager longing for the revealing of the children of God; for the creation was subjected to futility, not of its own will but by the will of the one who subjected it, in hope that the creation itself will be set free from its bondage to decay and will obtain the freedom of the glory of the children of God'' (Rom 8:19-21).

The gospel is not meant to be just a comforting story to tranquilize our fears. It is God's vision for the world's wholeness (another way of describing ''salvation''). To the degree that we live oblivious of God's program for cosmic transformation, we are like those who are already buried in the tomb. ''For those who live according to the pleasure principle (*sarx*: a self-centered, pleasure-driven vision of life) set their minds on the things of the pleasure principle (*sarx*), but those who live according to the Spirit set their minds on the things of the Spirit. To set the mind on the pleasure principle (*sarx*) is death, but to set the mind on the Spirit is life and peace'' (Rom 8:5-6).

The empty tomb of Jesus is an invitation for us to arise. Paul never wearied of exhorting his missionary churches to become signs of new life in their pagan world. The Letter to the Ephesians cites as a commonly known proverb: ''Sleeper, awake! Rise from the dead, and Christ will shine on you'' and then goes on to urge: ''Be careful how you live; make the most of the time'' (5:14, 15-16). The empty tomb is not the end, it is the beginning of the story of Christ's new life.

> *Lord Jesus, you have gone through the gates of death*
> *   into newness of life.*
> *Here death is present to us every day*
> *   in sickness, weariness, depression, lost opportunities,*
> *   and in countless aspects of diminishment.*

Yet you transformed human vulnerability
    by taking it upon yourself: ''becoming like your
    brothers and sisters in every respect'' (Heb 2:17).
We have said for centuries, ''what the Lord has assumed
    (taken up into his incarnate experience), he has redeemed.''
Allow us to live more deeply this mystery of our new life:
    even in pain and emptiness may your grace prevail.
    Make our struggle to walk in faith both light and peace for others.

THE
HOLY
SPIRIT

Jesus assured his apostles at the Last Supper, ''I will ask the Father, and he will give you another Advocate, to be with you forever. This is the Spirit of truth. . . . You know him, because he abides with you, and he will be in you'' (John 14:16-17). This grieved the apostles. Their master had just told them that he would soon be betrayed and that he would be leaving them. They could hardly comprehend the idea; they were just beginning to feel comfortable with their calling as his disciples. Their minds were filled with dreams of continuing the preaching and healing that he had taught them to do. They yearned for everyone to recognize Jesus as the worker of God's wonders, as they had come to see him. Now Jesus tells them that he must leave.

''Because I have said these things to you,'' Jesus continued, ''sorrow has filled your hearts. Nevertheless I tell you the truth: it is to your advantage that I go away, for if I do not go away, the Advocate will not come to you; but if I go, I will send him to you'' (John 16:6-7). Jesus explained that he must return to the Father and that the Spirit will come from the Father and the Son to transform the lives of those upon whom the Spirit will descend.

Jesus in this way gives us a new name for God: God is Spirit. God is breath, wind, breeze, inner movement of our hearts. This new name that Jesus gives to God evokes the most hidden movements of our own hearts. God is like this too, Jesus tells us; God dwells in depths of wonder and awareness too unfathomable to be expressed in ordinary words. God abides with us at the core of our being.

"When the Spirit of truth comes, he will guide you into all the truth" (John 16:13). Jesus' promise implies a profound transformation of the disciples through the gift of the Holy Spirit. The Spirit's witness is not described as a voice from the heavens nor a powerful outside force, but rather as the interior life which God lives within us. The truth of the Spirit is not a gateway to new information or new revelations. It is much more ordinary. The Spirit will guide us in finding the truth of our own being and destiny. "[The Spirit] will glorify me, because [the Spirit] will take what is mine and declare it to you" (16:14). The mystery of our hidden life, hidden even to our own selves, gradually unfolds under the influence of God's Spirit.

Most people seem to spend a fair amount of time in soul-searching. A subtle dissatisfaction with the rhythm and significance of our lives that is not quite depression affects many of us. We often wonder what is the use of our efforts and our projects. Encouraged as we are by the popular culture to make our own egos the frame of reference for our self-evaluation, we can find ourselves feeling empty and useless. Without the guidance of Jesus' Spirit, we can miss the truth of our lives. The Spirit's life within us makes our lives a procession of light and blessing; we carry God to all the corners of our days.

St. Paul, in his Epistle to the Galatians, tried to describe the effects of the presence of the Spirit in the lives of believers. "The fruit of the Spirit is love, joy, peace, patience, kindness, generosity, faithfulness, gentleness, and self-control" (Gal 5:22). Persons living by the power of God's Spirit are deeply attached to the divine love from which their lives proceed, contented and trusting in the wisdom and providence of God, generous and benevolent toward others as children of God, and accustomed to seeing the turbulence of daily affairs in the perspective of the mystery of life's origin and eternal destiny. God's life in us—the life of God's Spirit—helps us accept the transformation of our being according to the paschal mystery of Jesus. Dying, rising, and reanimating the forms of our earthly existence are the dynamics of this resurrection life we share.

The image before us shows the Spirit in the form of a dove flying out of the hand of Christ, who reaches out of the cloud of God's presence. This drawing condenses much of the mystery of God into a single picture. It evokes a strong feeling of action as the Spirit descends from the hand of the Son who extends the love of the Father to the world. The artist's intuition of the ever vivifying action of God in creating, in forgiving, and in guiding, articulates a truth that is at bottom simple, but demands much explanation to get it right.

When the Gospels tell the story of Jesus' baptism, they follow his coming up out of the water with his vision of "the Spirit of God descending like a dove and alighting on him" (Matt 3:16). The Spirit is presented as the source of transformation which remakes the human creature into a vessel of God's dynamic presence in the world. Jesus is empowered by the presence of God's Spirit to effect divine acts through the gestures of his human body. This is the role of the Spirit—to engender at the core of our being works of grace that will flow harmoniously into every dimension of human thought and operation.

In Paul's rich teaching on the Holy Spirit in his Epistle to the Romans, he uses an instructive phrase. "When we cry, 'Abba! Father!' it is that very Spirit bearing witness with our spirit that we are children of God" (Rom 8:15-16). This is another way of saying that God works in us in a fashion completely coherent with our personal freedom. St. Augustine in his *Confessions* used a phrase which is helpful in understanding what is at issue here. "God is more intimate to us than we are to ourselves"[14]—a strange thought, but correct. For this "intimacy" is the interiority of the gift of life constantly offered and the touch of animating love never withdrawn.

In invoking Jesus' Spirit, the Church has prayed for centuries this familiar prayer: "Come, Holy Spirit! Fill the hearts of the faithful and set burning within them the fire of your love . . . and you shall renew the face of the earth." The feeling of a full heart comes from the recognition that we cannot be loved any more plentifully than we are loved by God's Spirit. The Spirit anoints our powers by making us aware that we are inextricably bound to the holiness of ultimate Reality, that we belong to God's story of love for the world. The gift of the

Spirit melts our frozen hearts, alerts our failing senses, and lifts up our fading spirits. God needs us—the whole of ourselves—to be fully alive to the world. If only we could learn the song of the Spirit and teach it with patience and grace, then we could see God renew the face of the earth.

Spirit of God, be here now
    to heal and forgive, to make us live
    as radiant spokes in the wheel of life.
Take our hands and guide them
    in learning gestures of peace and compassion.
Patiently tutor our hearts
    that seek you in love's tabernacle.
Calm our fretful busyness; soothe our weary brains.
Beckon to us until we meet you
    in the cave of the heart.
And there teach us all things—justice, compassion, love—
    until we walk in righteousness and live in joy:
    witnesses to the presence of God in the world.

THE HEART OF GOD

The sentimental imagery of Valentine's Day cards, showing bright red hearts pierced by arrows, alludes to a deep reality of human experience. We yearn for soul mates—for heart-felt sympathy with others who will share the secrets and the story of our own hearts. Although we become vulnerable when we invest in relationships that move us to confide the dreams that drive our hopes, we never lose the instinct to do so. The communion that self-revelation makes possible is so great a prize, we find ourselves yearning for it despite the possibilities for disappointment and deception.

In each human life, there is some tale about betrayal and rejection. It takes time and experience to learn that harmony in love can result only from a process of tuning hearts that is as patient and delicate as tuning the strings of a musical instrument. All sorts of difficulties can get in the way. Infatuation prompts us to idealize the objects of our affection. But usually the recipients of such treatment are less than happy to be defined by another's fantasy about their identity and gifts. Maturity in relationships is arrived at only gradually, seldom without pain.

Poor social adjustment and even mental illness can be related to a person's failure to achieve a realistic appreciation of his or her significance in the lives of others. The ground-breaking American psychologist Carl Rogers created a formula for "client-centered" therapy that used a technique of "unconditional positive regard" or acceptance in order to establish a climate within which emotionally wounded persons could make a new start in a relationship of trust.[15] Rogers described his attitude in therapy as "active listening." This is a form of exchange in which the therapist reflects back to the client a statement which mirrors the client's ideas and feelings. Rogers discovered that most of his clients were so unused to being listened to sympathetically that his active listening became a momentous event in their lives.

As client-centered therapy proceeds, it becomes evident that the building of a relation of trust is more healing than any information that arises out of therapeutic conversations. Little by little, a fearful or rejected person comes to know what it feels like to be valued and prized by another. Once this breakthrough occurs, the patient can risk moving toward others in conversation and friendship.

This discussion of client-centered therapy may provide a context for special insight into one of the great mysteries of the Christian faith. The Letter to the Hebrews describes the Lord Jesus in the following way: "For we do not have a high priest who is unable to sympathize with our weaknesses, but we have one who in every respect has been tested as we are, yet without sin" (4:15). A significant part of the Christian good news is that God has come in Jesus to be with us and befriend us. Our healing and our empowerment arise out of our amazed acknowledgement that God has called us from isolation and fear into a friendship based on communion and care. "Zacchaeus, hurry and come down!" (Luke 19:5). "Follow me, and I will make you fish for people" (Matt 4:19). "Come to me, all you that are weary and carry heavy burdens, and I will give you rest" (Matt 11:28).

God is able to speak to us in Jesus and say, "Come—follow me," precisely because God has taken up our human heart—become one with us in our presence to this world and established a link with our humanity. Jesus is the embodiment of God. In becoming embodied, fully human while fully divine, the Son of God concretely expresses God's vulnerability and accessibility to us by allowing us to know that his heart is moved with love and compassion. "When he saw the crowds, he had compassion on them" (Matt 9:36); "moved with pity,

88

Jesus stretched out his hand and touched [the leper]'' (Mark 1:41). God made the choice to transform human destiny not by a corrective act of main force, but by a compassionate act of sovereign freedom. Jesus invites us to become new by falling under the sway of his affection. We are transformed by his love.

The heart is the core of a person and the concrete symbol of one's whole moral being. When anyone is touched to the heart, that means that their whole life is affected and changed. When the disciples on the road to Emmaus finally understood that it was the risen Lord who walked with them, they expressed themselves in these terms: ''Were not our hearts burning within us while he was talking to us on the road . . . ?'' (Luke 24:32). St. Paul speaks of the transformation of the believer that occurs when the Lord enters within us: ''May Christ dwell in your hearts through faith, as you are being rooted and grounded in love'' (Eph 3:17). The heart is where the realization dawns that we are cherished, understood, and loved.

The symbolism of the lancing of Jesus' side on the cross, therefore, is profound. In the sacrament of Jesus' body we see revealed the full expression of God's self-gift to human creatures. ''One of the soldiers pierced his side with a spear, and at once blood and water came out'' (John 19:34). Following St. Augustine, theologians of the Western Church interpreted this as a symbol of baptism (water) and Eucharist (blood) being derived from the sacrifice of the Lord on the cross. These sacraments of baptism and Eucharist of course are channels to the vivifying grace of God that transforms our human existence and lifts us up into conversation and communion with the divine.

Through these sacraments, God integrates into our lives the mystery that was revealed in Christ. By baptism, we are introduced into a pattern of living that finds new life and possibility after experiences of dying and diminishment. In the Eucharist, we are fed a transforming food that is the Lord's gift of his own life. Through these holy signs, God recognizes and responds to the pulse of our human rhythms of moral and psychological experience. We are constantly being threatened by various kinds of dying. When embraced with truth and humility, these moments can become occasions for a greater fullness of life. We are always hungry for a more definitive and convincing sense of meaning and significance. God feeds us with a share of the cosmic love that stretches out to embrace the whole world.

In the heart of God that pours forth healing water and nourishing life's blood for us, we meet the unconditional positive regard of God, who allows us to experience that we are received and understood. In Christ, God stands side by side with us in the dance of life, assuring us in all our ups and downs.

Here in our picture of the heart of God, the heart of Christ on the cross mirrors the holy, secret name for God, YHWH (drawn in Hebrew letters)—a name that pictures God as "that which truly IS" or "I am the One who I AM." This reminds us that at no moment can God stop loving us without our ceasing utterly to exist. All our *being* is from God. And we learn that this gift of *being* is not a cold, mechanical process, but a gesture of deep and understanding compassion. The heart of God, revealed on the cross in Jesus, is open to all, understanding of all, forgiving of all.

Our own hearts best know how to respond to this mystery of God's heart: "Create in me a clean heart, O God, and put a new and right spirit within me. Restore to me the joy of your salvation, and sustain in me a willing spirit" (Ps 51:10, 12).

> *Your grief is visible, holy God, in the wounded heart of Christ:*
> *your grief enfolds our tragedy, pain, failure, and the*
> *horror of cruelty.*
> *In the crucible of this sacred heart*
> *human misery is transformed by divine compassion:*
> *here is the sign of a love that makes whole the broken,*
> *that shares the unbearable—removes its sting.*
> *Lord Jesus, you teach us that we are linked—yoked—*
> *to the mystery of your heart lanced in death:*
> *"Learn from me: for I am gentle and humble in heart,*
> *and you will find rest for your souls" (Matt 11:29).*

TRINITY

Jesus showed us who and what and how God is. Some who heard him speak accused him of blasphemy. His idea of God was new, challenging, even frightening to them. John's Gospel reports certain listeners responding to Jesus in these words: "It is not for a good work that we are going to stone you, but for blasphemy, because you, though only a human being, are making yourself God" (John 10:33). For a Christian, God is defined in terms of the human life of Jesus, just as the full humanity of a believer can be defined only in terms of the Christian's relation to the God whom Jesus revealed.

What Jesus revealed about God not only brings God closer to us, but also introduces our own human experiences into the dynamic relation that the divine persons of the Godhead share among themselves. The doctrine of the Trinity is not abstract information about a distant God, but a river of life that constantly flows out and enfolds our own lives.

The Bible's account of the triune god develops gradually. The holy name YHWH—Giver of being, Creator of a people, Liberator of the elect—suggests transcendence, distance, and glory. While Old Testament theology is marked with certain expressions of God's love and compassion, it has created in Christians a false sense of God's inaccessibility.

The New Testament announces the one through whom a word of God will come in the opening lines of Mark's Gospel (the first writ-

93

ten of the four Gospels): "The beginning of the good news of Jesus Christ, the son of God" (Mark 1:1; cf. Rom 5:10; Gal 4:4). Having taken his disciples on a tour of preaching and healing, Jesus asked what people said of him. Then he asked, "What do you say?" Simon Peter responded: "You are the Messiah, the Son of the living God" (Matt 16:13). The disciples recognized Jesus as the one chosen by God to be Messiah, that is, the one anointed to perform God's own works in the midst of the people.

A clearer sense that Jesus is one with God comes from those episodes in the Gospels that represent the post-Easter understanding of the early Christian community. The New Testament stories of the annunciation, the infancy narratives, and the marvels surrounding the birth and childhood of Jesus explain Jesus as God's own child. Likewise, the baptism and transfiguration stories make it clear that, in the mind of the early Church, this Jesus of Nazareth is not only sent from God, but is also divine. It is the *kenosis* theme that becomes decisive in the preaching of the Church, reflected in the letters of Paul. (*Kenosis* means self-emptying.)

Paul instructs the early believers to have the same attitude that Jesus had, "who, though he was in the form of God, did not regard equality with God as something to be exploited, but emptied himself, taking the form of a slave, being born in human likeness" (Phil 2:6-7). This text summarizes the early Church's beliefs about the pre-existence of Jesus; Jesus as Christ has a relation with God that transcends time and space.

When we come to the mystery of the third person of the Godhead, we find that the disciples gradually grasp that the Spirit of God is not just the power of Jesus' resurrection reflected in the post-Easter Church, but a distinct manifestation of the deity within our world. Paul, speaking to the early Christians, tells them: "When we cry, 'Abba! Father!' it is that very Spirit bearing witness with our spirit that we are children of God, and if children, then heirs, heirs of God and joint heirs with Christ" (Rom 8:15-17). God acting personally within our personal lives is the Spirit of the Father and Son.

94

The Gospels too illumine the mystery of the Spirit of God. Jesus followed the leading of the Spirit who descended on him at his baptism in the Jordan (Matt 1:10; Luke 3:22) and guided him to the wilderness as he prepared himself for his public ministry (Matt 4:1; Luke 4:1). In his pastoral prayer in John's Gospel, Jesus describes the Spirit in this manner: ''When the Advocate comes, whom I will send to you from the Father, the Spirit of truth who comes from the Father, he will testify on my behalf'' (John 15:26). Here the relation of the Father, the Son, and the Spirit is summarized in the Gospel's own words.

This mystery is important for the Christian life. The Spirit of God (the Breath of God) is given to us to empower us to act on God's behalf. Jesus witnesses to life in the Spirit through his prayer, preaching, miracles, and obedience unto death. Jesus is ''raised in the Spirit'' to become a new creation open to all who believe. Jesus Christ becomes the ''first born within a large family'' (Rom 8:29) as through the Spirit Christians enter the relation of mutual love of the divine Trinity.

The breathing that marks our quieting down in meditative prayer is a symbol of the life of the Holy Spirit within us. God's breathing the Holy Spirit into us is constantly taking place. But when we enter a silence marked by the rhythm of slow, intentional breathing, we awaken ourselves to the reality of the Spirit, asking God's Spirit to instruct and guide us. The Spirit leads us through this quiet to the unfolding of God's word (heard in the Scriptures, shared in common prayer, studied in the gospel). The Spirit leads us from disharmony and chaos into an awareness of God's forgiveness and love. By the vehicle of this prayer within our hearts, we also breathe out our own spirit, offering our lives and ourselves to God.

Such prayer begins in the Spirit, awakens the saving power of the Son's word in our lives, and invites us to pour out our lives before the Father in adoration. We receive the breath of God and allow ourselves to be drawn toward God. This prayer develops our consciousness of being loved in Christ and of sharing life with all who are reborn as children of God. The spirit allows us to entrust ourselves back to the Father, accepting God's love and providence in our lives. By this mystery of contemplative prayer, we enter into the energy of mutual giving and receiving that is at the heart of God's hidden life.

Years ago, I made a retreat at Madonna House in Canada and met its foundress, Catherine de Hueck Doherty. Coming to the end of a pleasant conversation over lunch, she said: "So, you teach theology? And you came here to pray? You are always reading and writing, and when you're not doing that you're thinking, aren't you? Well now, go into the chapel, sit down, shut up! And let the icons pray for you!" This was an invitation to let an image like the drawing of the Trinity shown here orchestrate the hunger and the love of my heart.

This image invites us to recognize the powerful energy of the Spirit's movement in our lives. As our breathing becomes a metaphor for the inspiring presence of the Holy Spirit, we open our minds, our hearts, and our spirits to the indwelling of Father, Son, and Holy Spirit. Our prayer has as its goal neither to persuade God to respond to us nor to impress God with our righteousness, but to surrender to God, who has already redeemed us and loved us. Theologians for centuries and the Greek Church today call the Father's sending of the Son and the Holy Spirit a *perichoresis* (a Greek word meaning "dancing around"). This wonderful image suggests not only God's joy in togetherness, but a joyful sharing of divine life with us. This Trinitarian dance invites us to experience life as a relation of friendship with our God who never ceases to renew us in being, forgive us our weakness, and uplift and direct us on our path. The joy of this unceasing movement of hospitality and creation is the dance.

> *Source of all being, Light from whom all shapes proceed;*
> > *reveal your holy presence and make us holy*
> > *by touching us again with your life.*
> *May our spirits recognize your Spirit,*
> > *may our words speak of your Word,*
> *May our hearts rest even now in the peace*
> > *that is your eternal communion of love.*

96

PHYSICAL GRACES

God saw everything that he had made,
and indeed, it was very good.

Genesis 1:31

LIVING WATER

"In the beginning when God created the heavens and the earth,
the earth was a formless void and darkness covered the face of the deep,
while a wind from God swept over the face of the waters" (Gen 1:1-2).

These opening lines of the Book of Genesis echo an idea that was widespread among ancient peoples, namely, that there first existed a primitive mass of water from which living things came forth. To the eyes of our prehistorical ancestors, the undulating movement of the sea or the ripples on the surface of lakes suggested potency and fertility. Intuitively they recognized water as a powerful symbol of life, of renewal, and of healing. In the nineteenth century, this ancient notion of water as the primordial source of life found new expression in the theory of evolution, which saw the waters of the ocean as the breeding ground of the earliest forms of planetary life.

Today farmers know the complex power of water to transform the environment. Without rain, fields planted with crops will wither and die in the heat of the sun. Yet too much rain brings floods and sodden fields and a different sort of threat to crops. It is impossible to predict or to control the behavior of the rainfall. The best we can do is to plant our fields according to typical patterns of weather known from the past, and hope for nature to be gentle and cooperative.

The Bible celebrates God's power over the waters of the earth:

"You make springs gush forth in the valleys;
   they flow between the hills,

giving drink to every wild animal;
    the wild asses quench their thirst.
By the streams the birds of the air have their habitation;
    they sing among the branches.
From your lofty abode you water the mountains;
    the earth is satisfied with the fruit of your work.''

                                        (Ps 104:10-13)

The Church frequently uses water in its rites. Water gives birth, it washes and renews, it refreshes and cools, it slakes our thirst; it threatens death, but it can also lift up our bodies to float above the mysterious depths of potency hidden within its reaches. And water sings as well: gurgling over rocks in mountain streams, roaring with the breaking of the ocean's surf, dripping gently from above into quiet forest pools, and pattering rhythmically on the roof with its drops of rain. So much of our experience of life is condensed into the symbol of water that it is no wonder that water is the element used for the first of all the sacraments, baptism.

The Epistle to the Romans asks: ''Do you not know that all of us who have been baptized into Christ Jesus were baptized into his death? Therefore we have been buried with him by baptism into death, so that just as Christ was raised from the dead by the glory of the Father, so we too might walk in newness of life'' (6:3-4). Entering the waters of baptism is likened to falling into the depths of the sea, being swallowed up by its immensity, and yielding to its untameable power; the baptismal water is the symbol of death. But just as water can both give life and overwhelm with floodtides, so baptism becomes a new beginning of life even as it marks the ending of a previous kind of existence. ''For you have died, and your life is hidden with Christ in God'' (Col 3:3).

It is frustrating as well as consoling to see that in baptism God introduces us to new life by a form of communication that cannot be translated into a simple formula of words. Rather the rite uses the primal power of the natural symbol, water, to touch, refresh, wash, and enfold our lives in the sacrament of God's abiding with us through all the dying and rising that we will encounter in a lifetime. God embraces us in the water bath of baptism, marking our entire lifetime with the sign of everlasting life.

Baptism, like confirmation and holy orders, and normally matrimony, are sacraments that are not repeated because their grace continues to work in our lives; these sacraments *unfold* in us as our experiences lead us to awaken to the mystery of Christ's love. Certain moments of extraordinary insight, such as surviving a life-threatening accident or being awakened from crass blindness to the love of God (or the love of others), are like little baptisms that stimulate a new consciousness of the true shape of reality. Sometimes illness and forced rest will promote a reevaluation of life's meaning. That too is a kind of baptism, just as it is both a dying of a kind to familiar patterns of behavior and a rising to a new manner of living more responsibly and more gratefully.

The Book of Proverbs teaches: "The purposes in the human mind are like deep water, but the intelligent will draw them out" (20:5). Ultimately we come to understand the great respect that God has for each person. God waits until each of us in due time comes to understand the paradox of our existence. For all of us are absolutely dependent upon God's creative love to sustain our being, and yet God wills us to be autonomous and responsible for our own lives. We each have known both blessings and wounds, both love and cruelty; therefore God allows us to move slowly and gradually until we recognize the unquenchable benevolence that is God's care for us. We each know moments when we feel no need for help or support; thus God allows us to fall into other moments of emptiness and impotence that render us aware that we are creatures dependent upon God's power. Each time we are drawn out of the deep water of these human needs, we experience the power of our baptism. We are washed clean of illusions and given new life in faith.

One of the loveliest songs in the Bible is Psalm 1, which pictures God's faithful people as living in grateful awareness of God's constant mercies, symbolized by a flowing stream:

"Happy are those who do not follow
    the advice of the wicked
or take the path that sinners tread,
    or sit in the seat of scoffers;
but their delight is in the law of the LORD,
    and on [God's] law they meditate day and night.
They are like trees planted by streams of water,
    which yield their fruit in its season,
    and their leaves do not wither.
In all that they do they prosper."

God's gift of creative love, upholding us in existence, flows steadily into our lives. We are nourished by this faithful stream of life-giving grace until at last our faith blossoms into love.

When life rushes by like a running brook
    out of control: too full, too fast,
Gracious God, let us experience the peace that comes
    when our energies flow into a deep and tranquil pool.
We need to know the comfort of the serenity
    that lingers quietly over the hidden abyss
    of hope, of love, of gratitude.
Your grace, good God, is living water in our lives
    flowing into every part of our being.
You know more fully than we ourselves
    all that lies hidden in the secret pools of our yearning.
Teach us to be more patient,
    draw us into tranquillity,
    reveal to us the abundance of your love.

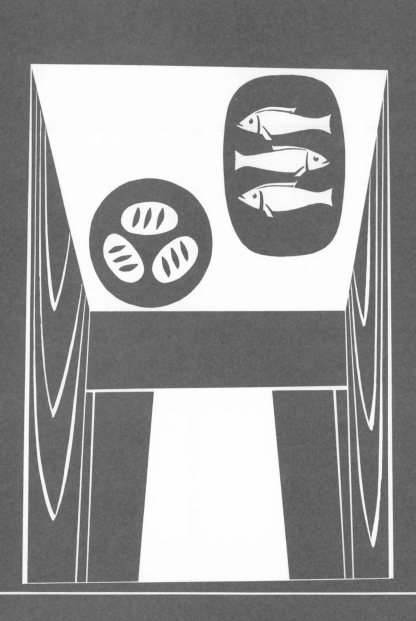

THE
TABLE
OF THE
LORD

God calls us to table and we find an abundance that surpasses our expectations. Like those who sought Jesus out in the wilderness, we sometimes do not realize how hungry we are until it is too late to find satisfaction from ordinary sources. We can imagine that God is put off by our neediness, when in truth our being has been finely crafted so that our inexhaustible hungers will lead us to the only source that can completely fulfill their yearning. To be human is to be hungry. To admit that we are hungry is to begin a journey to communion with God.

Mark's Gospel tells a story about Jesus feeding crowds who had come out to hear him preach. The people were hungering to be with Jesus and to enjoy his presence. So many people were coming and going that Jesus decided to slip away with his disciples by boat to a deserted place to "rest a while" (6:30). But many in the crowd saw Jesus make his escape. They guessed where he was going. So they hurried on ahead of him, arriving on foot before Jesus and the disciples got there. Out of compassion, Jesus again began to teach them.

"When it grew late, his disciples came to him and said, 'This is a deserted place, and the hour is very late; send them away so that they may go into the surrounding country and villages and buy something for themselves to eat'" (Mark 6:35-36). But Jesus responded to the disciples by telling them to prepare the people for a meal. He had them sit down in groups. Then he took all the food that was available—only five loaves and two fish—and blessed it and gave it to the disciples to offer to the people. "And all ate and were filled" (6:42).

This text radically connects the gift of Jesus' teaching and the gift of heavenly food. We need to be nourished and built up both by wisdom and by the holy feast which we share with our divine host. Over and over, Jesus shows us in the gospel that God wants to share life with us through readily available elements of ordinary life. Jesus' first miracle produced a mysteriously tasty wine for friends and their guests at a marriage feast in Cana (John 2:1ff). The father of the prodigal son lay on a banquet with the fatted calf to celebrate that his son had "returned to life," that is, reentered the circle of love and community on which he had turned his back before. In these stories Jesus shows how profoundly accessible God is in signs that are part of everyone's life: in our sharing of the table of friendship, in our mutual respect for one another in the rites of hospitality and recognition, and in our spiritual delight in the abundant gifts that sustain our physical and social well-being.

In John's Gospel, after the story of the multiplication of the loaves and fish Jesus gives a lengthy teaching about what constitutes real life. The people, clearly attracted to Jesus, want to be reassured that he is from God; they ask for a sign, like the sign that Moses gave them of manna in the wilderness (John 6:30-31). Jesus responds in terms of their example: ". . . the bread of God is that which comes down from heaven and gives life to the world" (6:33). And then: "I am the living bread that comes down from heaven. Whoever eats of this bread will live forever; and the bread that I will give you for the life of the world is my flesh" (6:51).

For most people, the pleasures of the table are significant symbols of human completeness. If we can afford it, going out to a fine restaurant is a special way to celebrate life-marking events—an engagement to be married, a reunion with an old friend, an anniversary, a promotion at work or some special success. If the emphasis at table is more on quality rather than quantity, we may go away from such an occasion savoring elegant, memorable aromas and tastes. One of the privileged ways that we move friendship beyond words and chatter is to sit down together to share such delights. It is a sign of respect and attachment that we choose to reach a deeper level of interpersonal relation in "breaking bread together."

Jesus uses this same human sensibility to express the promise of eternal life. He tells us that he is bread for us—"my flesh is true food and my blood is true drink" (John 6:55)—and that he gives us intimacy, affection, and friendship in the Eucharist. This bread, given at the table of sacrifice, makes possible our entering into the life of the one who places his life in our hands.

The Eucharistic bread and the cup of salvation are mysteries that belong as fully to our life beyond death as to our present life. They are already our sharing in Jesus' new life: "Drink from [this], all of you; for this is my blood of the covenant, which is poured out for many for the forgiveness of sins. I tell you, I will never again drink of this fruit of the vine until that day when I drink it new with you in my Father's kingdom" (Matt 26:27-29).

As with the disciples on the road to Emmaus, Jesus' gift to us of the bread blessed and broken is a sign that opens our eyes to the reality of a scope of life beyond our power to understand: "When he was at table with them, he took bread, blessed and broke it, and gave it to them. Then their eyes were opened, and they recognized him; and he vanished from their sight. They said to each other, 'Were not our hearts burning within us while he was talking to us on the road, while he was opening the scriptures to us?' " (Luke 24:30-32).

We come to the Lord's table on Sunday hungry for God and hungry for reassurance that we are loved. We hear God's word and sing our praises. This reawakens the power of our faith for us. We raise our eyes to the table as gifts are brought forward for the feast of life. And once again, gifts given by the hungering crowd who have gathered to hear Jesus' teaching are laid upon the table to become the communion of bread and wine.

God takes and transforms the bread and wine we offer. It is a sign of ourselves that we lay upon the table of this feast, whether it be in the form of bread or in the form of money. This is a moment of a holy exchange. The words of Psalm 116 are touching in this context: "What shall I return to the LORD for all his bounty to me? I will lift up the cup of salvation and call on the name of the LORD" (116:12-13). The desire to offer something lovely in thanksgiving is ancient; the means to do so are ordained by God: we offer back the same signs of life that we have received.

God gives us the bread of life, a nourishment that transforms those who eat it. The Eucharist is the food that makes us become the body of Christ. "Now you are the body of Christ and individually members of it" (1 Cor 12:27). We enter the mystery by love, never fully understanding what this new life means, just as we never fully understand the meaning and the enormous yearning that mark our everyday living. With all those who believe in this mystery of Christ, we become "members of the same body, and sharers in the promise of Christ Jesus through the gospel" (Eph 3:6).

The Eucharist table is our paschal banquet—our passover meal preparing us for our journey beyond the earthly life we best understand and strive so hard to control. Yet our lives are destined for a future life which is hidden to us. Slowly we grow in understanding and trust as we experience through our prayers and our faith a continuity of love and communion with those who have died.

The priest used to say to each communicant in the Roman rite: "May the body and blood of our Lord Jesus Christ keep you unto everlasting life." That is still the meaning of our communion. It makes us one with the Risen Christ; it strengthens us to live our lives as a witness to his reality. It is the first course of the banquet of life that Revelation promises us will be our everlasting joy: "Blessed are those who are invited to the marriage supper of the Lamb" (Rev 19:9).

> *You never ask from us at any time, gracious God,*
> *more than we can give;*
> *Yet you always ask of us to be a part of your feast,*
> *present and partaking in the banquet of true life.*

This festival is a celebration which is truly yours
*   but ours as well:*
It takes place in heaven and on earth,
*   in your heart and in our hearts.*
Help us always find ourselves in the sacred signs
*   upon the table of the Lord:*
Help us to believe and understand that we are changed
*   just as fully as the bread and wine.*

CANDLES

Lighting a candle sets the stage for festivity, whether in religious rituals or at a dinner table. I can remember my childhood feelings of expectancy when the altar servers came into the sanctuary of my parish church to light the candles before Sunday Mass. Their old-fashioned torches were designed to reach up high toward candelabra placed at the back of ornate, tiered altars. The glow of those candles in the half-darkness, just before the church was flooded with electric light, signalled that holy rites were about to begin.

Candlelight creates an atmosphere of reverence that symbolizes recollection and attention. In Catholic religious practice, tapers and vigil lights express personal devotion at shrines and when placed before images of Christ, his mother, and the saints. For people whose attention span at prayer may be brief, the burning candle prolongs the intention of our prayers even after we have left the scene. Such devotions are deeply rooted in our religious sensibilities. At shrines like Lourdes and Guadalupe, the many lights unite people who may not even share a common language. Candles and vigil lights before icons are at the heart of Eastern Christian piety. The cumulative effect of dozens or even hundreds of votive candles burning together witnesses to the corporate faith of many devotees, even though each flame was ignited by an individual in private devotions.

An intensely important moment in Catholic worship comes at the Easter Vigil when, after the blessing of the paschal candle which represents the Risen Christ, each person receives a wax taper that is lighted from the flame just blessed. As hundreds file into the darkened church carrying lighted tapers, the mystery that all of them bear Christ-life within them is made visible in the flickering lights. This moment is an inspiring sign of the powerful effect of many individual lights gathered in force.

In many places it has again become customary at Vespers on high feasts or Sunday evenings to repeat this ritual of sharing the flame of the paschal candle. Many oriental churches have never lost this symbolism. It reminds Christians that their whole life is illumined by the radiance of Christ's resurrection. He is the light of our life. As in the Easter Vigil, this service of light also symbolizes the direction and guidance that comes from the Lord as his light leads the assembly into the space of celebration.

Some years back, while visiting in western Kenya, I observed a fascinating use of candles and lanterns at the edge of Lake Victoria. Near midnight, fishermen there set lamps out on floats well off shore. These small lights attract insects and the agitated insects attract fish, which gather in great numbers for an impromptu feast. Then just before dawn, the fishermen trawl with their nets to round up the fish and bring them into shore.

From afar, the small lights glimmering on the water create a festival spirit. One would not easily guess their purpose. Yet as one draws closer, it becomes clear that they are the center of intense activity. There is a sort of optical magnetism that a flame in the darkness projects that changes the dynamics of the blackness and the stillness of night. Creatures are drawn more urgently toward the radiance and warmth of light, it seems, when the surrounding world is concealed in shadows.

Psalm 27 celebrates the power of light in these lines: ''The LORD is my light and my salvation; whom shall I fear? The LORD is the stronghold of my life; of whom shall I be afraid?'' (v. 1). Many people are accustomed to pray with a small candle burning in front of an image of Christ or a saint. It is hard to describe the comfort and the nourishment of these moments. The soft flame exerts a gentle attraction; its golden warmth enlivens the features of the holy image. The narrow focus of the small circle of light shuts out other concerns. The slight flicker of the flame brings a kinetic sense to the encounter. The burning wax is a constant offering, slowly and patiently expended. It amplifies and protracts the thoughts, words, songs, and feelings that arise in a time of prayer. All this expresses the love and trust described in the psalm.

Yet we cannot forget the Lord's words, ''No one after lighting a lamp puts it under the bushel basket, but on the lampstand, and it gives light to all in the house'' (Matt 5:15). However comforting and healing our own personal experience of the light of faith may be, our devotion is meant to generate compassion and generosity. This is what Jesus modelled for us. In privileged moments of intimacy with God, we should remember the breadth of Jesus' self-understanding: ''I am the light of the world, those that follow me will have light'' (John 8:12; 9:5); and to us: ''You are the light of the world . . . let your light shine before others'' (Matt 5:14, 16).

> To feel the enchantment of candlelight
>> we have to extinguish the artificial lights we have made.
> To become mindful of your unceasing benediction, gracious God,
>> we must withdraw from the clamor of our surroundings.
> Lord Jesus, teach us to do what you yourself did:
>> to withdraw and listen to your Father's silence,
>> to care passionately about your kingdom
>> of justice and love, of peace and light.
> Make us authentic images of your light,
>> crisp as a mirror reflecting your radiance.
> ''Let the light from on high dawn upon us.''
>> (Luke 1:78)

INCENSE

Fifty years ago, a Trappist writer used the image of burnt-out incense as a symbol of contemplative religious life. This image represented the extremity of self-sacrifice that he saw as characteristic of religious dedication. His book recounts in detail the privations and hardships that the first Trappists endured in coming to this country in the early years of the nineteenth century. The ordinary trials of pioneer living were intensified for them by the fasts, vigils, and poverty of their way of life. Their lives were all used up—burnt-out—in the project of implanting monastic life in the new republic, so unfamiliar with their way of life.

Changing cultural perspective from then to now, it seems appropriate to transpose this same metaphor of religious generosity from its former application to monastic life alone into the wider context of the Christian life as such. In doing so, we shift focus away from the burnt-out cinder and toward other dynamics of an extremely rich and ancient symbol of religious devotion. The key idea remains relevant to both scenarios: the offering of incense in prayer fittingly symbolizes Christians' response of love and dedication to God.

Before the Second Vatican Council, Catholics of the West were governed by minute rubrics concerning the use of incense in their liturgies. Since then, Church regulations regarding incense in public liturgies have become more flexible. Now incense may be used in any liturgy at the discretion of the celebrant. The manner of sending this fragrant smoke aloft may vary according to circumstances. Our drawing reminds me of the beautiful practice in some monasteries of placing incense in a large bowl and letting it burn throughout the liturgy of Sunday Vespers, mirroring the phrase of Psalm 141, "Let my prayer arise before you like incense, the raising of my hands like an evening sacrifice" (v. 2).

The use of perfume, incense, or scented oils to consecrate a space for worship as a sign of welcoming God into a sanctuary is an ancient practice. In driving away foul odors, incense symbolically chases away evil influences. Exodus describes in detail the rites for offering incense to God before the ark of the covenant in the meeting tent (Exod 30:7f; 40:5). There are ambivalent aspects in the smoking incense, since the same sweet-smelling cloud can function as a revelation of God's majesty and a concealing of God's presence. The power of this symbol is its eloquence in evoking the shifting dynamics of our experience of God.

There is an appealing text in the sayings of Ben Sirach where divine wisdom is made to proclaim: "Like cinnamon and acanthus, I have yielded a perfume, like choice myrrh, have breathed out a scent, like galbanum, onycha, labdanum, like the smoke of incense in the tent" (Sir 24:15). Here the joy of tuning one's understanding to the mysterious wisdom of God is compared to the pleasure of being surrounded by exotic, pleasant, and fragrant scents. It is easy to imagine a parallel with the garden of Eden, where the man and the woman walked and conversed with God in the cool of the evening amid the aromatic blossoms of the garden, and everything "was good" (Gen 1 and 2; esp. 3:8f). Something ancient within our nature yearns to recapture the harmony and delight that pertain to a right relation with our Creator by offering back to God the precious and uplifting gift of incense.

In the Roman Mass, the priest addresses the congregation at the beginning of the Eucharistic Prayer with the exhortation: "Lift up your hearts." The image of lifting up our hearts, our prayers, and our offerings symbolizes our desire to reach beyond the familiar frame of time and space and enter into God's presence. Even a cursory glance at

116

Christian ritual language will indicate how frequently the Church uses this imagery. This is why the visual metaphor of the cloud of sweet-smelling incense rising up in the middle of the people gathered in prayer is so moving. It is an emphatic statement about a deep yearning of our hearts.

John's Gospel tells the story of Mary, a friend of Jesus, who anointed the Lord at a banquet held at the house of Lazarus her brother, the one whom Jesus raised from the dead. Mary poured on Jesus' feet a whole pound of costly, perfumed ointment as a sign of love and respect, and then she wiped his feet with her hair. "The house was filled with the fragrance of the perfume" (John 12:3). This extravagant gesture aroused negative reactions in some of those present, who said that the money spent on the ointment should have been given to the poor. In response, Jesus said that this anointing was preparing him for his burial. In another Gospel he said that wherever the gospel is preached, this act of love will be remembered, using the same phrase as at the supper table over bread and wine, "in memory of her" (Mark 14:9).

We recall that after Jesus' death, women friends brought per-fumed oils and fragrant spices to prepare his body for burial. This was not just a remedy for the odor of putrefaction, but a sign of honor and love. In the Mass of Christian Burial Catholics incense the coffin of the deceased both as a sign of reverence for a departed loved one and a reminder of the person's destiny to be united with Christ in resurrection life. This sign is powerful and comforting. The cloud of incense rises to signify our yielding the one who has died over to God and our own self-surrender in a moment of pain and regret.

Every life is marked by loss and gain. Even the good and the happy will know disappointment and suffering. Some lives are tragic for the frequency or the magnitude of their grief. But everyone will know illness and pain, misunderstanding and alienation, and finally the renunciation of action and power. We must learn that we are more than what we do. Our life's meaning is rooted in trust. St. John of the Cross wrote, "In the evening of life, we shall be judged on love."[16] In the midst of torment, Christians keep their eyes on the cross, which is God's ultimate sign of love and the gateway to resurrection life. Incense, the fragrant, lovely substance that allows itself to be consumed and to float off into indeterminate space beyond our reach, signifies the loving entrustment of our lives to God's providence.

In the end, the metaphor of burnt-out incense remains telling. Every Christian's growth in faith will be accompanied by struggles that demand surrender to a hidden, mysterious providence. We give over control to God, often not understanding why great sacrifices are asked of us. This is a surrender of our own way, a capitulation of ego—of willfulness—that renders us more concretely aware of who we are and who God is. This entrustment of our lives and well-being to God is our self-oblation, lifted up sometimes in pain and struggle, sometimes in simplicity and freedom. The smoke of incense ascending is a token of our self-transformation in radical trust. It is a sign of a love stronger than pride, a joy deeper than success.

All that I am, all that I have—
    all is your gift, loving Giver of life.
Why was I so slow to acknowledge
        that what I thought was mine
        was your bestowal of goodness, of love?
Why am I still so grasping, so insecure,
        so dizzy when I recognize that I am not God
        (not even a little god)?
Grace has taught me your love,
        a love beyond telling:
        all is grace.
Let my prayer and my thanksgiving,
        my joy and my surrender,
        arise before you like incense.
Holy . . . holy . . . holy Lord!

BREAD

In a striking moment of overstatement, a liturgist friend of mine once said to a large audience: ''Never let a priest near an altar who has never made a loaf of bread!'' His point was that the presider at the Christian Eucharist ought to be vividly aware of bread both as ritual food and natural symbol.

Bread, just by being bread, is a forceful symbol with many dimensions. The Eucharist is not meant to exclude those dimensions, but to elevate them into the service of the breaking of the bread in Jesus' name. Just as bread delights us not only with its nourishing energy and wholesome taste, but also with its lovely shape and alluring smell, so likewise the Eucharist touches our lives not just with divine food, but with forgiveness and healing, intimacy with God and consolation.

Making and baking bread is a marvellous lesson in transformation. Dusty flour is so different from a moist, chewy bread; formless ground wheat is so different from a burnished crust. The moment when the yeast in the dough begins to resist the action of being kneaded into a loaf is a lesson in what it feels like for life to enter a lifeless lump of foodstuff. The rising, shaping, and baking of bread is an education of sensibilities that reaches well beyond its important lessons in chemistry. Bread-making shapes our understanding of beauty, purity, integrity, and wholesomeness.

However, sandwiches apart, Americans are not great bread-eaters. It is usually only on special occasions that most people here would find themselves looking for a bread knife. Our most typical form of bread comes already sliced into thin uniform pieces and wrapped in brightly colored plastic wrappers. To anyone accustomed to European or Mediterranean bread, this stuff is anemic indeed. I sometimes wonder what visual image most people have when they say the words of the Lord's Prayer: "Give us this day our daily bread."

Of course, those words of the Lord's Prayer have a scope of meaning beyond the literal sense of a loaf or a piece of bread. The "bread" of the prayer is everything that we need to sustain our physical life and well-being, something Jesus knew when he was tempted in the desert and said: "One does not live by bread alone, but by every word that comes from the mouth of God" (Matt 4:4). But just as in the Middle East bread really is the staple food eaten at every meal (like rice in the Orient, pasta in Italy, or potatoes in Ireland), so in the symbolism of the Bible and in the Christian liturgy bread has a universal meaning of great significance.

We are reminded that bread is the fruit of the hillsides. Isaiah, in promising God's blessings on Israel, says: "He will give rain for the seed with which you sow the ground, and grain, the produce of the ground, which will be rich and plenteous" (30:23). Many times the early Church at prayer recaptured this kind of earthiness when they prayed: "Just as wheat scattered on the hillsides has become for us one bread, so may we who eat this bread of life become one in the mystery of Christ." And we ourselves now pray in the Eucharistic Prayer, after the memorial of the institution of the Eucharist, "Grant that we who are nourished by his body and blood may be filled with his Holy Spirit, and become one body, one spirit in Christ."

Would not our enthusiasm for this mystery, which evokes our destiny to become signs of God's nourishing presence in the world, be greater if we had the daily experience of tasty, good bread that prompts salivation and anticipated delight? Would not our sense of the Eucharist as the center of our Christian lives be more vivid if we could recognize the family dining table as the extension and further realization of the Eucharistic table?

In recent decades, many people have begun to react to the form and shape of the bread, called "hosts," that had become traditional in Roman Catholic liturgy in recent centuries. Church officials' insistence that nothing but flour and water alone should be used in making these hosts meant that they had little potential to be appetizing. For centuries they were made of white flour, round in shape—a symbol of "otherness" and of purity, but to no one's eyes a familiar symbol of bread and all that the natural symbol of bread connotes. It has been observed that it took more faith to believe that these hosts were bread than that they are the body of Christ. Since the Second Vatican Council, people have become more sensitive to the mystery that the Mass is a meal shared with God, and more eager for the bread used to appear ordinary and familiar.

There are, of course, reasons for restricting the ritual bread of the Eucharist to unleavened bread, as the Western Church's disciplinary law requires. (Eastern Christians use yeast in their Eucharistic bread, employing a different symbolism.) Exodus not only prescribes unleavened bread for the night of Israel's flight from Egypt—to save time in their rush to get away safely (Exod 12:8f)—but also goes on to prescribe that each year there should be a memorial festival to celebrate the night of passover: "Seven days you shall eat unleavened bread" (12:15). The Christian liturgy's linking of the sacrifice of the Lord and his Eucharistic meal to the Passover meal inclines toward sympathy for using an unleavened ritual bread.

St. Paul adds to the argument. If unleavened bread is the bread of the Passover meal, it is a symbol of newness and readiness. Leaven, by contrast, expresses old habits and past mistakes. So, using these metaphors, Paul tells the Corinthians: "Clean out the old yeast so that you may be a new batch [of dough], as you really are unleavened. For our paschal lamb, Christ, has been sacrificed. Therefore, let us celebrate the festival, not with the old yeast, the yeast of malice and evil, but with the unleavened bread of sincerity and truth" (1 Cor

5:7-8). But alas!, neither Paul nor Exodus tells us their recipes for unleavened bread. We can hardly imagine it to have been tasteless, however.

These interpretations of the bread used for the rite of the Eucharist make us more aware of bread's expressive symbolic scope. It is a wonderful thing when those who are celebrating a special event can be invited to make or take part in making the Eucharistic bread. In the offertory rite, the bread for the Eucharist is meant to be brought through the assembly in procession as a symbol not only of the gifts which the people have brought to the table, but also as a sign of the way in which the gifts brought to the altar represent all that is ordinary and good in the lives of the faithful present.

Vatican II's constitution on the Church teaches in its chapter on the laity: ''For all their works, prayers, and apostolic endeavors, their ordinary married and family life, their daily labor, their mental and physical relaxation, if carried out in the Spirit, and even the hardships of life, if patiently borne—all of these become spiritual sacrifices acceptable to God through Jesus Christ. During the celebration of the Eucharist, these sacrifices are most lovingly offered to the Father along with the Lord's body.''[17] These are our ''daily bread'' in the fullest sense, which we receive each day from our Father in heaven and which we lovingly offer back in union with Christ at the Eucharistic table. This exchange of gifts, which ends in our receiving Christ's own body and drinking his blood, is the rhythm of our own transformation. ''Because there is one bread, we who are many are one body, for we all partake of the one bread'' (1 Cor 10:17).

> LORD Jesus, you made yourself to be living bread,
>   a food to sustain us on the journey to everlasting life;
> You placed this holy seed of divine life in the hands
>   of those whom you loved, so that they could share
>   the fullness of life that you received from the Father.
> Now you ask us to be a bread of life for one another,
>   to place our lives in one another's hands.

124

So we ourselves become one bread, one body
   in the power of your Holy Spirit.
Be the bread of our journey through life and our hope:
   ''for those who eat this bread shall live forever;
   and I shall raise them up on the last day.''

THE ROCK

The seventh chapter of Matthew's Gospel contrasts the image of someone who builds a house upon sand with someone who builds upon rock (7:24-27). When the rain falls, when floods come, when strong winds blow, one house collapses while the other weathers the storm because it rests solidly upon rock. Those who listen to the words of the Lord are like those who build upon rock. Their foundation is solid.

These images evoke the changes that affect our own psychological and spiritual lives. We have times when we feel as if our lives are about to fall apart, as if built upon sand. The pressures of overcommitment, too much ambiguity, divisions of opinion, pressures from important persons around us, and the like can lead us to feel that life is too much for us. We are insufficiently grounded. Everything feels as though it is going to fall apart.

The question of being grounded is an important one. In some ways it is typical for our age. We are, after all, the first generation to be instructed by the popular culture never to have an undistracted moment. So many homes have their television sets on whether people are watching or not. There are radios in automobiles; radios on the Walkman as people are exercising or strolling in the streets. This culture of overstimulation can distract us from inconvenient difficulties or duties. Ultimately its effect is to scatter our forces, leaving us feeling empty in difficult moments, used up, and without profound resources.

The Bible makes it clear that this is not exclusively a modern problem. Over and over the psalms invoke the Lord as the Rock. God is called a citadel (Ps 62), a rampart (Ps 31), and the Rock of our salvation (Ps 95). David, who is credited as the principal author of the psalms, as general of Israel's army and later its king, was frequently under attack. Centuries before as immigrants in an ancient land, and in David's day as an embattled minority, the Israelites frequently felt themselves in need of protection against powerful foes. This image of God as their Rock was an important one, encouraging and comforting them, reassuring them of eventual victory.

For us this image connects with another theme of perhaps greater significance. Today the very idea of God is problematic for many people. Many people approach the mystery of God solely in terms of early experiences of church or preaching or family devotions. Quite often these experiences have given them a sense that God, as proposed by parents or preachers, is a projection of wishful thinking, an imagined cosmic force meant to reassure us in the face of things in the world that frighten or dismay us. To affirm God in this fashion is to demean themselves, they fear.

Philosophers are in part responsible for the confusion about God in the popular culture. At the time of the founding of our country in the eighteenth century, many writers referred to "the Supreme Being" as the foundation for our enterprise of building a new nation. The very idea of a supreme being is problematic, because it places God in the same category as the beings that we see all around us. The words suggest that God is like things in our world, only somehow higher and better. This is fundamentally confusing.

The Bible does not speak of God as a superior entity in competition with creatures. God is rather the originating source of all things. Today theologians frequently speak of this mystery by referring to God as the ground of being. Trying to prove the existence of God—a problem posed to young people as they begin their university days—is a fundamental error of method. God does not so much exist as provide existence out of the fullness of divine reality. God is Reality.

128

This idea allows our imagination to think about God in a new way. The concept of a ground of being implies that whatever is thrown into existence rests upon a foundation that is essential for its reality. All that is, is upheld in being. God is, in this way, truly a Rock for reality, *Being* itself but not "a being."

Following this emphasis upon the categorical finality of God's reality, in terms of which all other reality is experienced as derived or borrowed, we recognize that our human and moral experience is ephemeral and contingent. If God is eternal, we are conditioned by time and change.

This drawing of the Rock expresses the power of these ideas. Shaped like a mountain, this rock touches the sky. It is able to bridge our experience of weakness with divine strength, our experience of vulnerability with divine power, and our experience of limited focus with divine purpose and vision. The Rock is also a center around which are gathered lesser features of the landscape. Ancient cities and villages were often built around a geographical prominence with a monastery or castle visible upon the hilltop and the village houses clustered at its base.

Such a rock functions as a center of gravity. Just as in gravitational theory the center is a force of attraction drawing to itself entities of lesser weight, so the image of the Rock in the Bible functions as a symbol of people being drawn to the presence of God. A beautiful text from the prophet Isaiah celebrates the pilgrimage of devout Jews going up to the feast in these lines: "You shall have a song as in the night when a holy festival is kept; and gladness of heart, as when one sets out to the sound of the flute to go to the mountain of the LORD, to the Rock of Israel" (Isa 30:29).

The New Testament also uses the image of the Rock as a symbol of attraction. A letter once attributed to St. Paul speaks of Christians becoming citizens with God's saints, no longer strangers, "built upon the foundation of the apostles and prophets, with Christ Jesus himself as the cornerstone. In him the whole structure is joined together and grows into a holy temple . . . in whom you also are built together

129

spiritually into a dwelling place for God'' (Eph 2:20-22). Not only are believers attracted to the mystery of Christ through the power of the Lord's Spirit, but they are called to be signs themselves—a kind of spiritual prominence in the social landscape—made new by their relationship with Christ in grace. ''Come to him, a living stone, though rejected by mortals yet chosen and precious in God's sight; like living stones, let yourselves be built into a spiritual house, to be a holy priesthood . . .'' (1 Pet 2:4-5).

God understands our vulnerability. Far better than we ourselves, God is attentive to the shifting sands of our human condition. Yet we are given a secure foundation. Christ Jesus is the Rock upon which we are grounded. There is never a moment when we do not have contact with the Rock who is our origin and our strength. Just as the stream of water flowed forth from the rock at Meribah when the Israelites journeyed through the desert (Exod 17:6-7), so the energies of our days flow forth from this rock that is our foundation and our strength.

This imagery invites deep serenity. Thought of or not, God is always present, always accessible to us. Perhaps it is also true that God, our Rock, invites us into a spiritual adulthood where, as we become more mature, we become more and more rooted—attached—to the Rock who is our foundation. Our prayer becomes more implicit, more quiet, more taken for granted. At the same time, our confidence in God and our awareness of grace become more pervasive and effective in everything we do.

> Let us come to rest in the hiding place,
>   the cleft in the rock,
> where David hid from Saul, where Elijah fled Ahaz,
>   where Moses found shelter on the mountain.
> You want us to find refuge, God,
>   in the shelter of your strength;
> to know in the midst of our struggle for life and liberation
>   about this place in which our hearts can rest.

130

We rejoice in the Rock of our salvation;
*   we enter God's saving presence with thanksgiving.*

                                        (Ps 95:1)

Be the ground of our being,
*   the firm foundation of our lives.*
Let us know that no storm or trouble
*   can shake us loose from the embrace*
*   of your life-giving, loving care.*

THE CROSS OF GLORY

The cross is the dominant symbol of the Christian religion. From the beginning of the Church's life it was the key sign of identification with the Lord. One sees it in early Christian marble carvings and mosaics in Rome and elsewhere in the mediterranean world. There it is usually represented not under the aspect of the crucifixion, but rather as a symbol of triumph and glory. Even on Good Friday, the Church's Liturgy of the Hours celebrates the meaning of the cross in terms of its triumph: "We worship your cross, O Lord, and we praise and glorify your holy resurrection, for the wood of the cross has brought joy to the world" (Morning Prayer, antiphon 3).

The cross is understood by Christian faith as the passageway or door between our earthly experience with its vulnerability to sickness unto death and the new life which Christ won for us through his obedient, sacrificial death. As noted so often in these pages, the transforming power of Christ's Passover experience of death and resurrection is not applicable to the moment of our physical dying only, but also to every modulation of loss, transformation, and sacrifice that touches our lives. Even in the midst of pain, the believer can know the joy of victory because the greatest terror of all—meaninglessness—has been swallowed up by the all-embracing grace that is the fruit of Christ's resurrection life.

One of the most powerful sayings of Jesus in John's Gospel explains how we are to think about the cross. In his long nighttime conversation with Nicodemus, Jesus patiently explains who he is in terms of a familiar story of the Old Testament. ''No one has ascended into heaven except the one who descended from heaven, the Son of Man. And just as Moses lifted up the serpent in the wilderness, so must the Son of Man be lifted up, that whoever believes in him may have eternal life'' (John 3:13-14). Later in John's narrative of the last week of Jesus' earthly life, Jesus says, '' 'When I am lifted up from the earth, I will draw all people to myself.' He said this to indicate the kind of death he was to die'' (John 12:32-33). It was on the frame of a wooden cross that Jesus was lifted up both to suffer death and to conquer it.

Jesus' enigmatic saying about being lifted up presupposes a knowledge of Israel's Exodus journey and the incident of the poisonous snakes sent among the Israelites as a punishment for their grumbling. After many Israelites died, the people came to Moses and asked him to obtain relief from the Lord. When Moses interceded for the people, the Lord said to him: '' 'Make a poisonous serpent and set it on a pole; and everyone who is bitten shall look at it and live.' So Moses made a serpent of bronze, and put it upon a pole; and whenever a serpent bit someone, that person would look at the serpent of bronze and live'' (Num 2:8-9).

This image says *healing*: ''Come here for healing!'' Today we expect doctors to bring about physical healing by surgical and pharmaceutical means. Sometimes people approach medical dispensaries with the same attitude that they bring to the auto mechanic. ''Find out what's broken and fix it!'' But Jesus' healing is not the same as fixing. What needs to be healed?

We need to be healed of our mortality: our walking toward death is the ultimate wound that each one of us carries even in the vigor of life. That wound touches us frequently with its shadow of sadness and regret, especially when somone dear to us dies. We also need to be healed of our spiritual vertigo—our loss of balance—when we lose track of the purpose of living. We need to be healed of the spirits of retaliation, envy, greed, manipulation, anger, and fear. We need to be healed of our unconsciousness of who we are.

The apostolic Church understood that. "You know that you were ransomed from the futile ways inherited from your ancestors, not with perishable things like silver or gold, but with the precious blood of Christ, like that of a lamb without defect or blemish. . . . You have been born anew, not of perishable but of imperishable seed, through the living and enduring word of God" (1 Pet 1:18-19, 23). This author goes on to say: "Once you were not a people, but now you are God's people; once you had not received mercy, but now you have received mercy" (2:10).

If we gaze upon the cross of Jesus, we shall find healing. Like the Israelites being cured when they looked at the image of what was about to kill them, we too can find life by recognizing the sign that God will not let either serpent or death itself eradicate our lives. Jesus draws all people to himself, since all alike are wounded with this pervasive wound of mortality; all alike need healing through new life.

The cross is the Christian's emblem of transformation. To raise up the sign of the cross is to create an atmosphere of grace. Within view of the cross upon which Christ gained victory over death, we gather in faith to hear the gospel word proclaimed, to sing our praise, to break the bread of thanksgiving, and to offer the gift of our lives to one another and to the mission of the gospel. The community that is Church gathers around the cross as a sign of hope.

Sadly we also have to acknowledge that many times this sign of the cross has been carried on imperial shields and military helmets. The cross was emblazoned on the crusader's breastplate and carried on the flags of troops throughout the centuries. The gospel arrived in the new world on ships that carried cross-marked *conquistadores* who came to shed blood in pursuit of gold and who violently coerced ancient peoples to be baptized before they could be led to understand the mystery of Christ's revelation. Although the cross is the instrument of the triumph of Christ over death, Christian triumphalism has too often made it for non-Christians a symbol of violence, betrayal, and greed. We cannot allow ourselves to forget how easily we yield to the temptation to manipulate the lives of those weaker than ourselves.

135

Yet this cross is the sign of Christ's love and of God's mercy. "For God so loved the world that he gave his only Son, so that everyone who believes in him may not perish but may have eternal life" (John 3:16).

Perhaps, after all, St. Paul is the most eloquent preacher of the cross. "For Christ did not send me to baptize but to proclaim the gospel, and not with eloquent wisdom, so that the cross of Christ might not be emptied of its power. For the message about the cross is foolishness to those who are perishing, but to us who are being saved it is the power of God" (1 Cor 1:17-18). Paul bids farewell to the Galatians with these strong words: "May I never boast of anything except the cross of our LORD Jesus Christ, by which the world has been crucified to me, and I to the world. For neither circumcision nor uncircumcision is anything; but a new creation is everything" (Gal 6:14-15).

The raising up of the cross of Jesus and the inauguration of his Passover mystery were the inception of a new creation, a new world. This is clearly nonsense to those who would reduce life to nothing more than a calculus of physical and chemical forces. But to those who have known the power of God's love in Christ, the cross is wisdom and joy.

We meet our mortality in fatigue and sickness,
loneliness and fear, sin and despair.
And you, gentle Giver of eternal life, call out to us
to journey to you on the bridge that will carry us
beyond our limits, beyond our tested courage,
our voluntary oblation.
You have sent us your own beloved, the Splendor of your Glory,
in whom the fulness of your love was pleased to dwell.
This Son of Man showed himself like to us
in all things but forgetfulness, but ingratitude,
in all things but sin.
He climbed upon the ladder, the trellis, the scaffold
that bridges the unspeakable distance
between heaven and earth, fear and love.

This is the holy cross:
the instrument of death to dying and life in grace.
Bless our eyes, our minds, our flesh and bones,
bless our memory, our desires, and all our actions
as we look upon this emblem of your love and our salvation.

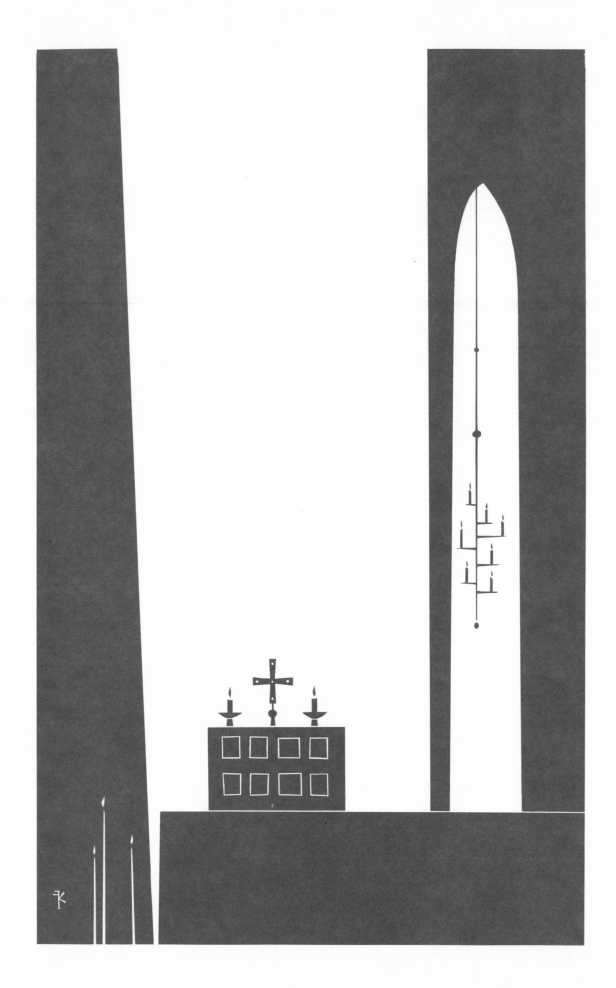

SACRED SPACE

During the nineteenth century, museums replaced cathedrals and religious shrines as expressions of culture and grandeur in much of Europe. Many former churches and monasteries were turned into museums, like Mont St. Michel in France, which is one of the world's greatest tourist attractions. Splendid environments like that which have endured through the centuries can elevate our feelings and affirm our faith. Words fail to express the bouyancy of spirit that a visit to such a place promotes.

Yet many buildings which once were expressions of faith and devotion for the people who erected them, have been wrenched out of their original context and secularized. The French revolution's violent turn against the Church was a decisive moment for modern history. Because Church officials had at times been instruments of a corrupt monarchy, the fervor of the revolutionaries in leveling all hierarchies led to the frenzied destruction of religious buildings. The results of this systematic vandalism are still evident to those who visit the monuments of western Europe. Yet the deeply felt urge of the human spirit for grandeur and transcendence did not disappear. It was channelled into a fascination with and a veneration for the arts.

Today our large American cities have palatial structures that serve as temples for the fine arts. Museum visitors make their pilgrimage to great paintings and sculptures, moving slowly and using reverent, hushed tones in the solemn atmosphere. Some of our finest buildings are museums. Inside them we can rightly learn valuable lessons about the human spirit.

Earlier in this century, many of the church buildings we built had as their chief value to remind immigrant parishioners of buildings or architectural styles from the old country. Often a scarcity of means dictated that efforts to replicate a Gothic cathedral or a Baroque shrine would produce poor results. Many of us were raised in religious environments of this sort. Moreover, when our turn came to take responsibility for producing new structures for the church in recent decades, our first inclination was to overturn the past, to reject the depressing, dark, cluttered, and homely environments of Victorian church edifices. Yet often this transition was achieved without a clear sense of positive objectives for renewal.

The Bishops' Committee on the Liturgy tried to guide the sensibilities of contemporary Catholics with its statement on *Environment and Art in Catholic Worship.* Their statement explains: "Because the assembly gathers in the presence of God to celebrate [God's] saving deeds, liturgy's climate is one of awe, mystery, wonder, reverence, thanksgiving and praise. So it cannot be satisfied with anything less than the beautiful in its environment and all its artifacts, movements, and appeals to the senses."[18] The beautiful is related to the numinous, that is, to a sense of the presence of the Holy. This quality is fostered by care in the making of objects destined for liturgical action and care in the selection of elements for worship. "In a world dominated by science and technology, liturgy's quest for the beautiful is a particularly necessary contribution to full and balanced human life."[19]

Sacred space is an environment which serves the high purpose of providing the meeting place between God and mortals. It succeeds when it achieves eminence of beauty and simplicity along with elevation of tone and feeling. The words of Jacob after awakening from his vision of the heavenly ladder suggest the power of such a place: "Surely the LORD is in this place—and I did not know it! . . . This is none other than the house of God, and this is the gate of heaven" (Gen 28:16-17). The Rule of Saint Benedict echoes this sense of the sacred in its instruction on the oratory: "After the Work of God, all should leave in complete silence and with reverence for God, so that a brother who may wish to pray alone will not be disturbed by the insensitivity of another"; and concerning the praying of the psalms: "We believe that the divine presence is everywhere and that in every place the eyes of the Lord are watching the good and the wicked."[20] A heightened sense of God's presence is the goal of sacred space.

Christian worship demands a space that serves both hospitality and contemplation. Worshipers should be able to see, recognize, and welcome one another. Likewise, they should all be touched by the sense that, like Jacob, they are in a place charged with the presence of God. "A simple and attractive beauty in everything that is used or done in liturgy is the most effective invitation to this kind of experience. One should be able to sense something special (and nothing trivial) in everything that is seen and heard, touched and smelled, and tasted in liturgy."[21]

Such space is sacred because it has been set aside to celebrate the holy mysteries of the Lord's incarnation, the memorial of his paschal mystery, and the action of the Holy Spirit in the community. The sense of holiness in the community's gathering place derives from the feelings of depth and authenticity that the community members have experienced in their worship together, followed perhaps by their silent and private moments of refuge from the clamor of the world. Liturgy is both personal and communal. Liturgical celebration must be characterized both by welcome and accessibility and by genuineness and respect for the symbols that carry the dialogue of communication and communion between the Church and the Lord.

In the lives of young believers, the impact of sacred space is considerable. The volume of space in the place of worship, the beauty of liturgical arts used for windows, sculpture, and ritual vessels, and the majesty of liturgical actions themselves landscape the religious imagination of the child. This esthetic influence colors the credibility of the religious message itself, contributing to the whole process that leads one to firm belief and to the integration of faith within the elements of a world view.

This heightened sense of fullness of feeling in a place of beauty set aside for God is evoked memorably by the psalmist:

"How lovely is your dwelling place, O LORD of hosts!
My soul longs, indeed it faints for the courts of the LORD . . .
For a day in your courts is better than a thousand elsewhere . . . O
LORD of hosts, happy is everyone who trusts in you" (Ps 84:1, 2, 10).

While we know that God wills us to bear the Holy Spirit within us as the fruit of our worship, making us "ambassadors for Christ" (2 Cor 5:20), we understand that we are still called to come aside to a quiet place and rest and ponder God's marvels (cf. Mark 6:31). In such a place, the echoes linger of God's word proclaimed and of the people's praises. Memories of the Spirit's visitation are linked to the loveliness of the place. This space is an unceasing offering of beauty and reverence to the Holy One.

> *Teach us the secret of finding eloquent expression*
> > *in the simple beauty of your silence and your presence, Lord.*
> *You are in our midst and that is all that matters.*
> *So we can quiet our urgent complaints,*
> > *quell the pressure of our obsessions,*
> > *and let our passion to explain melt away in love.*
> *Show us how to see your love in the simple signs*
> > *of reverence, graciousness, and peace.*

A WORLD OF BLESSINGS

So if anyone is in Christ, there is a new creation:
everything old has passed away;

see, everything has become new!

2 Corinthians 5:17-20

REDEEMING THE TIME

Space and time, two categories basic to our thought processes, are so central to our experience of reality that we cannot imagine a world without them. Yet that is precisely what biblical revelation challenges us to do. Since both space and time are expressions of our creaturely being, God invites us to a communion beyond these limits that the gospel calls eternal life. Can we live within time in a way that prepares us for a life beyond time? Can we redeem time itself?

The Church's liturgy is the celebration of our new life in baptism. In baptism we have already begun an existence that belongs to the realm of eternal life. In Scripture we find phrases which try to suggest what this might mean: ''For a thousand years in your sight are like yesterday when it is past, or like a watch in the night'' (Ps 90:4). Such a use of human language tries to wean us away from language's limits. It invites us not only to share God's life, but to prepare ourselves to share God's mode of being beyond space and time. The Second Letter of Peter warns us that God's Day ''will come like a thief''; it reminds us ''that with the LORD one day is like a thousand years, and a thousand years are like one day'' (3:8, 10).

There is no common measurement for time and eternity. In faith we enter a new and different reality, the reality suggested by the Lord's promise, ''where two or three are gathered in my name, I am there among them'' (Matt 18:20). This mysterious reality is achieved particularly when we gather in faith to celebrate the Lord's supper and enter the communion of Eucharistic love that binds us not only to those believers with whom we share the sacred meal, but to all of those who live new life in Christ.

From its earliest centuries, the Church has been aware that it must celebrate the saving work of the Lord in ways that will awaken in believers a recognition of redeemed reality. The mysteries of our redemption—the events in the life of Jesus Christ and the story of his death and resurrection—belong to all ages. The Church's liturgy makes these mysteries present in our own day.

As Vatican II's liturgical constitution states: ''Every week, on the day which she has called the Lord's day, [the Church] keeps the memory of his resurrection. In the supreme solemnity of Easter she also makes an annual commemoration of the resurrection, along with the Lord's blessed passion. Within the cycle of a year, moreover, she unfolds the whole mystery of Christ, not only from his incarnation and birth until his ascension, but also as reflected in the day of Pentecost, and the expectation of a blessed, hoped-for return of the Lord.''[22]

The drawing before us expresses something of the mystery of our living between two worlds, one of space and time, the other of promise and expectation. The letters *XP*, the first two letters of the Greek word for ''Christ,'' preside over the seasons of the year, symbolized here by the ancient signs for the zodiac. The word *zodiac* comes from Greek words meaning the circling or cycle of living beings. It symbolizes the constellations of stars in twelve segments of 30° each that are seen differently, month by month, in the changes of the seasons. The zodiac is one of the most ancient expressions of human concern for the measurement of time and space. There is evidence on ancient pottery from as early as 4,000 B.C. of drawings of figures suggested by the shapes which the stars trace in the nighttime sky.

For agricultural and seafaring peoples, the stars offered indicators of both geographical direction and the measurement of the seasons. Speculation about the influence of the stars on human destiny has kept the constellations a source of limitless fascination for the popular imagination. Already by 450 B.C., the twelve signs of the

146

zodiac were identified and recognized. The idea that the position of the stars as viewed in certain seasons might have an influence over human affairs led to the development of astrology and to uneasiness over the supposed power of heavenly bodies on human events. The medieval idea of the "wheel of fortune" refers to the rotation of the signs of the zodiac in the heavens and the vulnerability of people to the power of fate.

Christian faith, however, proclaims that God has raised up Christ to be a greater power than any on earth or in the heavens. "Christ is the image of the invisible God, the firstborn of all creation; for in him all things in heaven and on earth were created, things visible and invisible; . . . and through him God was pleased to reconcile all things, whether on earth or in heaven, by making peace through the blood of his cross" (Col 1:15-20). It is the work of liturgy and Christian life to bring this faith to expression in our daily lives.

With every first Sunday of Advent, we begin a new liturgical year. We make our way through four weeks of reading the prophets who foretell the coming of the Messiah. Following Christmas, we have several weeks of quiet delight in the mystery of God become man, until it is time to begin the long Lenten renewal that prepares the Church for Easter. We celebrate the resurrection mystery for fifty days until the feast of Pentecost, and then spend our summer months in leisurely reflection upon the Holy Spirit's fruitfulness in the life of the Church, until it is time to begin the liturgical year over once again.

Not only our months and our weeks are marked with these memorials of our redemption. Each day has its cycle of prayers to sanctify the time. These are readings and chants of psalms, Scriptures, and hymns to acknowledge the presence of God in our midst and remind us of the world beyond time and space, the world to which we move in faith. This daily "liturgy of the hours," as it is called, is principally the responsibility of monastic communities; but priests, religious, and many lay people also participate in this "work" of the Church to praise and adore the eternal God and to intercede for the well-being of the world and for its safety and its healing.

147

The center of the church's liturgy is Easter—the Lord's Passover from mortality to eternal life. This Easter mystery also signifies our passage into the mystery of life beyond time and space. Jesus said: ''If I go and prepare a place for you, I will come again and will take you to myself, so that where I am, there you may be also'' (John 14:3).

Just as all the mysteries of Christian life take their energy from the resurrection, so all the events of the liturgical calendar are plotted in accordance with the one festivity that is astronomically calculated. Each year, Easter Sunday in the West is the Sunday after the full moon following the vernal equinox. This is the Sunday that follows the date of the crucifixion of Jesus. The rising of the Lord lies at the center of our faith and marks the unfolding of our days until this present experience of space and time opens out upon the new creation that is the unending Day of the Lord. Remember how Christ instructed the disciples to pray to his Father: ''Thy kingdom come!'' Each day, as we do this, we ask to enter the new, redeemed world that was revealed when Jesus was lifted out of death and made the Lord of everlasting life.

Holy mystery beyond our vision, beyond our reach—
beloved God—stay near to us.
Our days unfold in ups and downs, joy and weariness,
hopes and fears.
Redeem our waiting for your glory to be revealed,
and bless every action, thought, and desire as we wait.
Reach into the circle of days so like one another
and speak to us clearly of your love and of your will.
You are the Lord of time and space,
the gracious one who saves us from confusion and despair.
Lord of history, have mercy on us!

FAMILY

The normal path to holiness is through marriage and family life. Council theologians made the family a symbol of the Christian life in calling it the "domestic church" and describing it as follows: "Christian spouses, in virtue of the sacrament of matrimony, signify and partake of the mystery . . . which exists between Christ and his church. The spouses . . . help each other to attain to holiness in their married life and by the rearing and education of their children. And so, in their state and way of life, they have their own special gift among the People of God."[23]

The Catholic Church has suffered from the myth that married and family life is less holy than the life of priests and religious. This is really not a "myth," but an "anti-myth." No bishops, priests, or vowed religious in their right minds think anything like this anymore, yet the idea still lingers on among lay people. The Church's true attitude is expressed in these lines of a key statement of Vatican II: "The Lord Jesus, the divine Teacher and Model of all perfection, preached holiness of life to each and every one of His disciples, regardless of their situation: 'You therefore are to be perfect, even as your heavenly Father is perfect' . . . thus it is evident to everyone that all the faithful of Christ of whatever rank or status are called to the fullness of the Christian life and to the perfection of charity."[24]

Statements like this make us realize that we need creative images of holiness that describe the work of the Spirit in the lives of believers. For spouses and parents, holiness will not be achieved by long periods of silent prayer in some quiet environment. Their holiness will be in the patient and faithful exercise of their duties and their generous concern for each other. Parents are the first preachers of the faith to their children and the ones responsible for modeling healthy, authentic life. They are responsible for leading their spouses and their family to the peace and happiness of knowing that they are loved by one another and by God. The Church comes into being within the family, even before it does within the parish church assembly. The family is not only the cradle of physical life but the cradle of faith as well.

The Catholic Church insists that matrimony is a special sacrament in which Christ's saving action in the Church is made visible in a particular way that helps couples to encounter God as a source of life, forgiveness, and holiness. As spouses accept their responsibilities to one another and their families, they are guided by the gift of the Holy Spirit. The special grace of this sacrament makes God's love and assistance available to them precisely as they accept the duties they have taken upon themselves. They fulfill their call to holiness as they accept the challenges that pertain to growing in intimacy and generativity— that is, growing in responsibility to one another and to their children.

The unusual drawing symbolizing family is surmounted by the cross. Living any form of community is painfully difficult in our tumultuous society. It is daunting to enter into a commitment to respect, intimacy, and generous mutual concern within the context of family life. Parents rarely control the atmosphere within which their relationships with one another and with their children develop. Coming to know and love one another with deep concern is a great difficulty in so frenetic a world.

A major goal of family life is the couple's growth in intimacy. Matthew's Gospel recalls a word of Jesus which is both a challenge and an encouragement to the couple: ''Have you not read that the one who made them at the beginning made them male and female, and said, 'For this reason a man shall leave his father and mother and be joined to his wife, and the two shall become one flesh?' So they are no longer two, but one flesh. Therefore what God has joined together, let no one separate'' (19:4-6). This image uniting the couple body and spirit as a single moral personality is the great ideal of marriage. The obstacle is the individual egoism of each of the spouses.

The late psychologist Erik Erikson described true intimacy as one of the milestones of adult human development. In intimacy an individual learns to respect and love another not according to his or her fantasy of how the other ought to be, but according to the real, precious, unrepeatable reality of that unique other person. When couples achieve intimacy, there is a confidence and a radiance to their relationship which can be a powerful witness for others.

In similar fashion, Erikson describes generativity as another major transition in adult growth. Through generativity, the couple open up their lives to a wider world than the immediate relationships of their own family. As children bring others into the family circle, they extend the experience of all the members of the family circle to different values and cultures. At the same time, healthy adult parents open their lives in friendship to wider circles of experience and cooperation. Generativity might be described as the virtue that welcomes difference, sponsors the talents of others, and brings about the situation where members of a younger generation are able to enter confidently into their own creativity. Family thought of in this way is a holy institution, mirroring the love and creativity of the divine Creator.

A touching incident in the gospel shows Jesus receiving the little children of those who heard him preach. The disciples appear to have been indignant at wasting the master's time in this way. But Jesus said: ''Let the little children come to me; do not stop them; for it is to such as these that the kingdom of God belongs'' (Mark 10:14). This passage makes us reflect that not only is the family an image of Church, but also an image of God's kingdom. The theme of the kingdom of God is grace: we are all children of a loving God. We all belong. Yet Jesus did not have a sentimental understanding of family life, otherwise the powerful story of the prodigal son in the fifteenth chapter of Luke's Gospel would not be what it is. Jesus understood about jealously, the slow awakening of youth to responsibility, and the anguish and solicitude of parents for their children's well-being. It is because of such realism that other New Testament images for marriage and family life are so powerful.

In chapter five of the Letter to the Ephesians, an analogy occurs that has proved important for the Church's theology. The writer explains that husbands and wives enter into a union in married love which is a symbol of Christ's union with the Church. So he exhorts wives and husbands to love one another as a part of their very selves. "For no one ever hates his own body, but nourishes and tenderly cares for it, just as Christ does for the church, because we are members of his body" (Eph 5:29-30). Today theologians describe marriage as a covenant between partners rather than a contract. For centuries theology was inclined to use the latter term, making marriage appear to be a legal or juridical relationship in the eyes of the Church. But no one reading Ephesians could come away with the idea that the early Church's notion of matrimony was a legal affair. Rather, the sacrament of matrimony is a symbol of the Church's own reality. The Church visibly appears when spouses in Christian marriage grow into a covenant of mutual respect, intimacy, and generativity, making a sign in the world that God is committed to the human community through Christ. The family is a sign of what the Church is, a community of love living in the Holy Spirit.

Because family is the privileged realization of the life of the Church in day-to-day reality, its duty is to extend to its members and to the world around it the gifts of loving service that marked the life of Jesus. Because of the characteristics of the family circle as well as their vocation to witness to the gospel, a Christian family is the seed and the sign of a community of love that can change the world.

Jesus gave as his new commandment, "love one another as I have loved you" (John 15:12). Children first learn the meaning of this divine command in the family. The power of grace heals the wounds of ordinary troubles in family life and urges members on to their full maturity and growth. The family is the foundation of society and the

154

heart of the Church. There is no more difficult vocation in the Church than living the responsibilities of married and family life with integrity and grace. This vocation extends to parents and children across generations. It calls forth their deepest generosity and offers them the possibility of transforming for good the world around them. It is a challenge which is also a blessing.

Lord Jesus, you grew in age, wisdom, and grace
> *in the care of Mary and Joseph.*
Your hidden years of family life
> *sanctified the times and seasons of our households.*
We make our way through the journey of living together
> *in an adventure of risk and discovery.*
Give us the grace to respect the particular beauty,
> *the unique spirit, of our companions in life.*
May our forgiveness convey your own divine pardon,
> *may our love be full enough to channel godly love.*
We pray for abundance of life, joy, and love:
> *let us share it widely and wildly*
> *in imitation of your love for the church.*

ANGELS

"The Most High will command the angels concerning you
    to guard you in all your ways.
On their hands they will bear you up,
    so that you will not dash your foot against a stone."
(Ps 91:11-12)

God's providential care to sustain the well-being of creation—
especially the well-being of us human creatures—is evoked in these
lines from the psalms. This particular psalm is one of the most frequently repeated in the monastic Liturgy of the Hours, appearing in
the night office of Compline for Sunday and feast days. The spirit of
this psalm is set out in the opening lines: "You who live in the shelter
of the Most High, who abide in the shade of the Almighty, will say to
the LORD, 'My refuge and my fortress; my God, in whom I trust!'"
(91:1-2). God invites believers to trust in divine love and care.

The figures of angels come and go in the pages of the Bible as an
expression of God's hidden power being exercised in the midst of our
visible world. The Old Testament used the Hebrew word *malak,* translated as "angel" or "messenger of the Lord," to signify an action
willed by God that touched the lives of humans. Two angels came to
Lot in Sodom to warn him and his family against God's destruction of
that city (Gen 19:1-23). An angel of the Lord called to Abraham just as
he was about to sacrifice his son Isaac (Gen 22:11). God sent an angel to

watch over the people of Israel and to guide them in the Exodus journey to the Promised Land; God told Moses, "Listen to his voice . . . for my name is in him" (Exod 23:21).

As recorded in the New Testament, the life of Jesus was marked by intimate association with angels. Mary, his mother, received her call to virginal motherhood through the annunciation by the angel Gabriel (Luke 1:26-38). At the conclusion of his temptation in the desert, Jesus was visited by angels and comforted by them (Matt 4:11). During the agony in the garden of Gethsemani, "an angel from heaven appeared to him and gave him strength" (Luke 22:43). Jesus spoke of angels as real and active beings: "Take care that you do not despise one of these little ones; for I tell you, in heaven their angels continually see the face of my Father in heaven" (Matt 18:10).

In the perspective of the Bible, over and over again angels mediate communication between God and the people. When God has a message to share, angels are the mysterious figures who bear the news. The angel Gabriel gave the promise of miraculous births both to Zachary and to Mary (Luke 1:19; 1:26). A multitude of angels celebrated the birth of the savior with praise and song (Luke 2:13-14). Likewise, angels announced the good news of the resurrection of Jesus (Matt 28:5; Mark 16:5; Luke 24:4; John 20:12). The thought world of the Bible envisages vast numbers of heavenly beings that accompany us and surround us, guiding and protecting us against the "cosmic powers of this present darkness, against the spiritual forces of evil in the heavenly places" (Eph 6:12).

Theologians of the third and fourth centuries, trying to understand more fully the mysterious identity of these messengers of God, drew upon ideas of ancient Greek philosophy to explain their understanding of angels. Thus the early Church imagined angels as intelligent, immaterial creatures who belonged to a hierarchy of being superior to ours. Because their understanding is not limited by material conditions, by time and by space, the angels can comprehend in a single simple intuition all the fullness of truth that we only gradually and partially struggle to know. They are beings of truth and love who serve as mediators between the divine and the human both because of the nobility of their nature and because of their mission to assist us humans.

The depicting of angels in art is a curious phenomenon. Angels are characteristically shown with wings, since (like birds) they are thought to inhabit the heavens. The ancients' idea of divine beings inhabiting the heavens or high mountains (like the Greek deities on Mount Olympus) also favored flight as a symbol of supernatural or divine origin. Other ancient peoples (such as the Assyrians) also used winged figures to represent supernatural beings. Baroque art sentimentalized the image of the angel, filling religious sculpture and paintings with figures of cherubs as cute, fat little babies with wings, inadvertently provoking the hard-headed skepticism that eighteenth-century rationalism developed regarding any phenomenon that can't be seen or felt or measured.

By an ironic twist of fate, contemporary physics is struggling to deal with phenomena that astronomers consider essential for explaining the nature of the physical universe, even though these phenomena cannot be detected by any conventional means of scientific measurement. James Trefil, a physicist, describes the situation like this: ''Dark matter is strange stuff. It's all around you but you can't see it. It's whistling by your ears but you can't hear it. It is arguably the most important material in the universe, but until recently scientists had no idea that it existed.''[25] He is describing one of the key ideas of contemporary astronomy. The mass of the clusters of the heavenly bodies in the galaxies exceeds the sum of the mass of the individual heavenly bodies. The experienced gravitational force of heavenly bodies can be explained only by recognizing that the space between stars and planets is not empty, even though we cannot visually detect anything there. It is filled with ''dark matter''—a force whose effects we can recognize, but whose identity remains a mystery.

The function of angels in Christian theology is not altogether different. In addition to the little that is explained about angels in the many texts of the Bible where they appear, angels represent the filling up of the spiritual universe with loving essences that mediate the omnipresent care and love of God for all creatures. Perhaps instead of calling them "dark matter," we might reverse the analogy and call them "light matter"—beings of light. The problem with that, of course, is that the theological tradition has claimed that they are not "matter" at all. They are immaterial—without atoms, molecules, time, or space. But they are parallel to dark matter in the sense that in the spiritual world, it is hard to explain the blessings of providence without their loving action on behalf of the world.

I have a friend of a mystical bent who is fond of saying that a coincidence is just an everyday, ordinary miracle for which God prefers to remain anonymous. It may be as apt to say that it is an ordinary miracle mediated by the graced intervention of an invisible angelic presence. Some theologians nowadays attribute the presence of angels in the Bible as readily to cultural thought patterns as to a decisive will on the part of the Scriptures to categorically affirm the existence of angels. As one theologian recently summarized it, while angels are certainly *in* revealed texts, it is not obvious that their existence is the significant content *of* the revealed texts.[26]

One attribute of angels that is striking in the drawing presented here is the dimension of adoration. The angelic forms that we are considering are shown hovering about the throne of God. This is an allusion to the imagery of the Book of Revelation where the multitudes of angelic spiritual beings are drawn into the on-going liturgy of praise and thanksgiving that is the overpowering psychic event of eternal life. "Day and night without ceasing they sing, 'Holy, holy, holy, the LORD God the Almighty, who was and is and is to come'" (Rev 4:8). Their pure openness to the spiritual intelligibility of God's infinite truth and beauty elicits from them delight and thanksgiving and adoration before the throne of the Holy One. Their presence near to us mediates the holiness of that heavenly liturgy.

Perhaps our drawing is the best summary of this complex reality. The little village is serene, wrapped in the peace of the evening's stillness. Hidden to the eyes of the people there, God's blessed spirits attend—ministers of care and providence. The angels are likewise engaged in the mystery of the court of heaven even as they attend to the needs of their earthly charges. The scene inspires confidence in God's loving care, and serenity of heart. It also expresses the fuller mystery of our solidarity in love and in praise with all God's spiritual creatures. Peace be to all the creatures of the universe—seen and unseen—peace and love before the face of the Holy One who gives us life!

We acknowledge you, Holy God, as the source of life,
as our maker and as the master of our lives.
You call us into a communion of love
revealed to us by Jesus your Son—our brother.
By this same communion, you invite us to take part
with every spiritual creature
in your festival of life and creation.
Guide us by the blessed spirits whom you have sent
to cherish us and care for us.
May we become one with all those who worship you;
may we find energy and healing in their company.

EVIL

In the drawing before us, the relation between evil and the cross is evident. Not only is God concerned about the human situation, but on the cross God becomes enmeshed in the human predicament of sin and evil, and the son of God incarnated in human flesh suffers and dies. Yet the cross also overpowers the darkness. Sin and evil are the reason for the crucifixion and the context for the redemptive coming of God into human flesh. God's victory over evil leads creation into a new phase of redemption, making humankind and the world itself new realities through Christ's resurrection.

Jesus was an exorcist, one who identified the powers of evil and addressed them with such authority that he brought about new life for those enslaved by them. The Church still has an exorcizing mission. The Church must recognize the powers of darkness and identify them. They include the demons of militarism, nationalism, sexism, the greed of the unprincipled wealthy, consumerism, and hedonism. People must be liberated from enchantment by the false promises of any of these demonic sources. Much of what is stupefying in the popular culture (for example, the gross obtrusiveness of television advertising) is a celebration of the power of these demonic forces. It is exorcism when people are delivered from false views of social reality and from negative patterns of relating to one another. Even today, some evil can be cast out only by the power of God.

The New Testament shows us a Jesus who is not afraid to confront the power of evil. Yet the Church appears to hesitate in speaking about Satan, evil, sin, or demonic powers, since the popular culture mocks belief in devils. Still we ask each day in the Lord's Prayer to be delivered from evil. We are responsible for allowing ourselves to be seduced by the diabolical, whether that force is a devil or the demonic powers in the culture. But the cross is never far from our encounter with temptation. Just as Jesus was drawn by compassion toward those who were victims of demonic powers, so we can express the compassion of Jesus toward those who are afflicted with the demonic forces of our time—poverty, violence, racism, or drugs. We find ourselves in both segments of the image before us. We can recognize our connivance with evil as well as accept our vocation to be instruments of an exorcizing, liberating Christian love.

The twentieth century may contain humanity's most extraordinary experience of evil. Two world wars and countless other armed conflicts have marked this century as no other, in terms of the magnitude of human and physical destruction. It is even conceivable that we humans will be the agents of our own extinction, if not by weapons, then by the destructive effects of our technology. Genocide, violence, and pollution are part of the legacy of this century's progress.

Some people are disaffected from the Church because they feel that its preaching does not take evil seriously. Others cannot conceive of an all-powerful God who would allow the sufferings of this century—the shoah, or the gulags of Stalin's bloody regime, or the killing fields of Cambodia—to take place. What meaning can the concept "God" have in the face of such extravagant viciousness? It is an affront to men and women to believe in a God who is remote and disinterested in our human predicament. Who needs such a God?

For Christians, evil is closely related to sin. From a biblical viewpoint, sin is a break with God leading to a tragic separation of humans from the source of their life. Sin has no meaning for someone who has no idea of God or who does not believe that God's covenant with human beings is the most important event in human history. If someone lacks the concepts of sin, covenant, and providence, then the monstrous evils of our century represent a powerful argument against the

164

reality of God. But if one has learned to recognize God as the Giver of life, then the mystery of evil, while still incomprehensible, can fit into the wider story of God's ways with the world.

The evil that is mystifying is not so much the bad that *happens to people,* like floods, earthquakes, and disease, but the bad *that people do.* How can a God who brings about the reality that we know allow malevolence? Christians believe that God is responsible for the good that we do. We are not free in spite of God, but because of God. God is the source of my being and my actions, inviting me to enter more fully into the perfection of my nature (my kind of being) and thus into true freedom. We imagine that God can give a gift of grace that would forestall our doing evil without destroying our freedom. Why doesn't God always give everyone that grace? That is the great mystery.

The opening story of the Book of Genesis represents temptation in the form of a talking snake. The snake's symbolic significance is linked to its strange characteristics: it moves quickly without legs, it lives in holes in the ground, and it sheds its skin as it renews its life. It is also a powerful sexual symbol. The constellation of these attributes endows the snake with an aura of danger and elusiveness. It is such a creature that approached the first man and woman in the garden and, through deception and trickery, led them to betray their loving relation with their Maker-God.

The New Testament speaks of demons or unclean spirits. An unclean spirit attaches itself to the spirit of a person infested with a diabolical presence, so that everything that proceeds from that person's actions will be affected. In a number of passages we find Jesus expelling demons from troubled persons. Symbolically this teaches us that Jesus had the power not only to drive the demons out of individuals, but also to liberate people from the fear of the demonic or the unclean.

An important passage in the Acts of the Apostles tells the story of Peter and the centurion Cornelius who invited Peter to preach to his household and baptize them (Acts 10). Peter, troubled about inviting non-Jews into the Church, had a powerful vision in which he saw a large sheet lowered down out of heaven containing animals that were ritually unclean according to Jewish custom. As he looked upon this strange vision, he heard a voice from the dream tell him: "What God has made clean, you must not call profane" (10:15). One effect of the preaching of the gospel is the liberation of the world from senseless taboos. Old categories of clean and unclean—"we" versus "they"—are done away with. Christ has triumphed over evil as embodied in nationalism, sexism, racism, or any other divisive force.

We tend to blame outside forces for the evil that we do. The Genesis image of a tempter is still alive, if not in terms of a magical serpent, then in terms of neuroses, trauma, environment, or other compelling forces. In the days of Jesus demons were taken for granted. The point of the biblical text is not to teach us that such creatures exist, but to show us Jesus' power over every destructive force.

The magnitude of the destruction wrought by the wars of our century should not lead us to ignore the fundamental responsibility that belongs to human choices. Monstrous evil is more appalling when we reflect that human pride, megalomania, and chauvinism inspire prejudice and violence. But just as deformed moral sensibilities are the causes of this evil, so graced benevolence is the only remedy. We are redeemed from evil not merely by having pain and violence taken away, but by being transformed by grace to become agents of reconciliation and compassion.

Deliver us from our selfishness, our indifference, our isolation
and from the loneliness that weakens us to sin.
Deliver us from our fear of being unloved and unwanted
and from the weariness of working without faith or hope.
Deliver us from our unloveableness and our incapacity to love.
Deliver us from every evil, past, present, and to come.
Deliver us, O Lord, unto our brothers and sisters
in a genuine openness one to another.
Deliver us unto the experience of creation in a community of hope.
Deliver us unto our work with imagination and courage.

Deliver us unto the grace of loving one another
  exactly as we are.
Give us your peace, and through your peace in us
  give peace to all who meet us, all who see us,
  all who live in the support of our friendship,
  our love and our example.

THE CITY
OF
GOD

I am fascinated by the relics of the past. Few experiences move me more than a visit to an ancient city or ruin. Somehow the ideals and the hopes of those who built such places outlive the inhabitants and their society.

Once I wound my way through the narrow streets of an eleventh-century village in the south of France. It was afternoon. The golden-hued limestone of the Midi was glowing in the brilliant sun; the shutters of the houses were closed against the heat of midday. Each time I ducked into the shade or entered a covered walkway, the coolness of the old stones revived and refreshed me. After many twists and turns, I made my way to the heart of this village which originally was the extended community of an old Benedictine monastery. There, in the center, was the abbey church—a refuge from the heat, a space of silence and peace, a temple filled with the prayers of a millennium of saints. Inside I somehow felt the presence of countless spirits who had found in this very place rest, calm, and the presence of God.

The Bible proposes various descriptions of a heavenly city where the tensions and imperfections of our earthly life are supplanted by a peace and a harmony that are God's own initiative for our human happiness and our beatific transformation. The Book of Revelation describes this scene: ''I saw the holy city, the new Jerusalem, coming down out of heaven from God, prepared as a bride adorned for her husband. And I heard a loud voice from the throne saying, 'See, the

169

home of God is among mortals. God will dwell with them as their God. . . . God will wipe every tear from their eyes. Death will be no more; mourning and crying and pain will be no more, for the first things have passed away' '' (Rev 21:2-4).

At the heart of this vision is the message that God is near and dwells with the people in this city of joy. God's friendship and care change everything. The emptiness, restlessness, and violence that characterize life in our cities will disappear. Instead there will be rightness and fulfillment. The author of Revelation continues the description: ''I saw no temple in the city, for its temple is the Lord God the Almighty and the Lamb. And the city has no need of sun or moon to shine on it, for the glory of God is its light, and its lamp is the Lamb'' (21:22-23).

Elsewhere Revelation describes the heavenly liturgy that takes place at the end times: ''Then I looked, and I heard the voice of many angels surrounding the throne and the living creatures and the elders; they numbered myriads of myriads and thousands of thousands, singing with full voice, 'Worthy is the Lamb that was slaughtered to receive power and wealth and wisdom and might and honor and glory and blessing!' Then I heard every creature in heaven and on earth and in the sea, and all that is in them, singing, 'To the one seated on the throne and to the Lamb be blessing and honor and glory and might forever and ever!' And the four living creatures said, 'Amen!' And the elders fell down and worshipped'' (Rev 5:11-14).

The Church's doctrine of the communion of saints is built on the foundation of images like these. This apocalyptic vision makes of our ordinary life an apprenticeship for the mysterious fulfillment that is pictured here. Somehow the deepest currents of life in all of us— whether philosophers or accountants, artists or mechanics, managers or contemplatives—are the creative energies that arise not out of our own flesh and blood, but out of the unceasing generosity of a creator who is always recreating the universe.

Our redemption from sin is, in a certain sense, our redemption from the futility of merely rehearsing gestures in a drama without a plot. To the extent that we have no destiny but the self-involved betterment of our physical and intellectual life, we fall into the absurdity of expending our life's energy to make all our chasing around in circles more expeditious and comfortable. God did not intend us for a cosmic merry-go-round, but for a journey toward a home where life will be completely realized.

In this present life, we waste too much of our energy in an unconscious competition with God. Children go through a stage at about three or four years of age where they fixate upon becoming independent in manipulating complex objects in their environment. "Let me do it myself!" they cry, when an exasperated parent tries to take a dangerous or precious object out of their hands. This need to prove ourselves lingers much longer in the spiritual life. The inclination to achieve on our own and then seek approval and reward from God becomes a serious obstacle to growth in the spiritual life of the Christian.

The heart of a mature faith is the recognition that God is present and active in every dimension of reality. There are no sacred parentheses in which God hides from the world at large. All things manifest God's creative love. Each person and event bears witness to the action of God.

This is why St. Paul gives such importance to the image of the Church as the body of Christ. "For just as the body is one and has many members, and all the members of the body, though many, are one body, so it is with Christ" (1 Cor 12:12). God is continually renewing the processes of life and society, all the while calling us to be more sensitive to the foundational reality of love: we are not in competition with one another; we are meant to be mutually enabling members of one corporate existence.

Granted, this sounds like naive madness to hard-headed people in a commercial world. The industrial age began under the banner of the philosopher Hobbes, whose phrase "man to man is an arrant wolf"[27] later found its echo in Darwin's theme of "the survival of the fittest." Unwittingly we breathe in this atmosphere of rivalry, advantage, profit, and manipulation as we negotiate our way through the marketplace.

Ironically there is almost nothing in the late twentieth century that is designed to endure for a thousand years. Increasingly the profit motive has displaced the ideal of enduring beauty in favor of disposability and obsolescence. The entrepreneur gets his or her cut each time new goods are sold.

Yet cities are also places where the finest achievements of the human spirit are celebrated. People love to live in cities to enjoy theater, symphony concerts, sports events, museums, and art galleries. All these cultural enterprises help us to realize how much we depend on others for our own happiness. Most cultural achievements are the product of cooperation, demanding peer respect and mutual benevolence among collaborators to achieve something of enduring worth.

Perhaps some day our consumer culture too will pass to make way for another image of human society. Pope John Paul II in recent years has stressed the need for Christians to close the gap between faith and culture. "This will be possible," says the pope, "if the lay faithful will know how to overcome in themselves the separation of the gospel from life, to again take up in their daily activities in family, work and society, an integrated approach to life that is fully brought about by the inspiration and strength of the gospel."[28] Success at breaching the gap will involve creating a different vision of human relationships where beauty is more desirable than financial profit, friendship more precious than advantage, and solidarity in a common vision of human dignity more compelling than self-fulfillment.

The theme of the nobility of every calling was dear to Martin Luther. He wrote that the Christian life can be summarized in terms of faith and love, through which we are placed between God and our neighbors "as a medium which receives from above and transmits again through below. Like a vessel or pipe, [we] should act as a channel through which the fountain of God's gifts flows uninterrupted to nourish others."[29] Every estate in life, every calling is holy. The holiness of the city is in the mutual service and friendship of people conformed to God's love in Christ. Loving service to our neighbors is the norm of ethics in the Christian life.

This is the challenge contained within the image of the city of God. Like all apocalyptic visions, it affronts our customary ways of thinking. Yet a patient rumination on the promises of the city of God—peace, security, community with the saints, and joy in the presence of the Holy One—can open our hearts to recognize our deep yearning for fullness of life. "Death will be no more; mourning and crying and pain will be no more, for the first things have passed away. And the one who was seated on the throne said, 'See, I am making all things new'" (Rev 21:4-5).

You made us for life, not death, Lord God.
Yet so often we concentrate on distracting ourselves
    from the seeming dead end of dying.
Nonetheless you never stop asking us to imagine
    what life without dying will be.
Help us more and more to see the city of God
    not just as a promise for life beyond human events,
    but as your invitation even now to find life in your presence.
"God is love.
Whoever live in love live in God, and God in them.
In this way, love is made complete among us
so that we will have confidence on the day of judgment,
because in the world we are like God."
                    (1 John 4:16-17)

THE FOUNTAIN OF LIFE

Twenty years ago I was privileged to travel in India. My purpose was to lecture at several catechetical centers and to offer talks to groups of Catholics who live vowed religious life. To prepare, I spent a good deal of time reading up on the culture; I was particularly curious about the religious customs of the Hindu people and their ancient tradition of meditation and spirituality. But nothing I read prepared me for the wealth of wisdom that I encountered there.

I had read that religious Hindus find inspiration for their prayer in nature. Everywhere I went, their temples were built next to rivers, streams, waterfalls, lakes, or fountains. The sight and the sounds of moving water are metaphors for the presence of God in the world. The music of water—lapping, bubbling, rippling, dripping—is a language as eloquent as words, and often more compelling.

On the afternoon of an exhausting day of train rides, long walks, visits to ancient ruins, and sightseeing in museums, I came with my Indian companions to a small rural temple where a modest hillside stream flowed through a viaduct to end with a splash in a pool outside the shrine of a Hindu divinity. There in the temple garden was an elderly devotee rapt in meditation. I stopped in awe. The site was wonderful. Green plants in the garden were thriving, though outside the temple area the ground was crusted and dry. Bright blossoms graced the bushes, scenting the air with a soft fragrance that mixed with the smell of dust. And the fountain of water sang on.

In that place I learned a new language. Something inside me learned to say and sing exactly what the splashing water said. I closed down my observing, reflecting, describing, and judging and tuned in to a discourse about love and thanks—a discourse without words, without utterance. Sometimes our loving communion with the world can be articulated in the depths of our being better through silence than speech. In such moments we are truly graced, because there we learn to listen with the whole of ourselves. There every part of our being learns how deeply loved we are.

Jesus speaks about the fountain of life, using the metaphor of water as his invitation to trust in the power of life itself. In John's story, Jesus is resting while the apostles are in the city trying to buy food; they are in the midst of a missionary tour of teaching and baptizing. Jacob's well in the little town of Sychar was where Jesus rested, tired out by his journey (4:6). Speaking to the Samaritan woman at the well, Jesus offers to her a source of life that will change her being: ''Those who drink of the water that I will give them will never be thirsty. The water that I will give will become in them a spring of water gushing up to eternal life'' (John 4:14).

We know the story of how Jesus surprised and shocked this woman by telling her that he knew of her previous career: he invited her to trust him—to trust both his knowledge of her spiritual thirst and his ability to promise her transforming life. The well where the woman draws water offers the cool and refreshing liquid that is necessary to life. Jesus builds a parallel image of a well of love and power that is necessary for everlasting life.

Water imagery was vitally important to people surrounded by arid hills, dry valleys, and villages where every drop of water had to be hoarded. Water was life. But Jesus promises a new kind of life through the gift of a new source of water. Isaiah the prophet spoke in much the same way. Speaking for God, he said: ''Do not remember the former things, or consider the things of old. I am about to do a new thing; now it springs forth, do you not perceive it? I will make a way in the wilderness and rivers in the desert'' (44:19). ''Everyone who thirsts, come to the waters; and you that have no money, come, buy and eat! Come, buy wine and milk, without money and without price'' (55:1).

We have a thirst that arises from the core of our being, a hunger that is lifelong and worrisome. To be human is to be thirsty—thirsty for life, for friendship, for meaning, and for joy. Too often we interpret this restlessness and this thirst as an illness rather than as what it is— God's invitation to us to drink from the fountain of life. We are so little pleased by the rites of the Church, I think, because we fail to recognize the importance of this embarrassing thirst that afflicts our souls. We remain unaware that God means to slake our thirst with divine drink.

The final vision of the Bible is this powerful revelation to the seer John on Patmos: ''Then the angel showed me the river of the water of life, bright as crystal flowing from the throne of God and of the Lamb through the middle of the street of the city. On either side of the river, is the tree of life with its twelve kinds of fruit, producing its fruit each month; and the leaves of the tree are for the healing of the nations'' (Rev 22:1-2). The life of the triune God flows out from the throne of God at the heart of the heavenly Jerusalem. Its energy is offered to those who believe in God through the witness of the Lamb. This river is love that arises in God, life that flows from the throne of God, given to us by the Lamb in the power of the Holy Spirit. This is how we become life-giving presences, like the trees whose leaves are for healing.

We are sadly mistaken when we imagine that the river of divine life is meant exclusively for ritual moments, that it is a sort of divine commodity given to broken and empty people when they come to the sacraments. God's abundance is inexhaustible. The river is intended to be ''a spring of water gushing up to eternal life''; it is meant to flow in and through us all the time. But we fail both ourselves and the mystery into which Jesus invites us when we enter it on the condition of understanding and controlling everything ourselves. To be good conduits of the river of life, we must be empty of ourselves. To be empty, we must learn the music of the water and let its movement and sight and sound speak for the inarticulable yearnings in the depths of our being. Paul has it right: "we do not know how to pray as we ought, but that very Spirit intercedes with sighs too deep for words" (Rom 8:26).

In the beginning, the first man and woman were persuaded by the crafty serpent not to trust God who had forbidden them only the fruit from the tree that stood in the middle of the garden. When they took the fruit of that tree and ate it, "the eyes of both of them were opened, and they knew that they were naked" (Gen 3:7). They had learned "good and evil" (v. 5), they who had been created to know only goodness. From that moment, trust in goodness was humankind's great problem.

Many symbols merge. Those who are washed in the blood of the Lamb, who have entered the heavenly Jerusalem, live next to the river of the water of life and become fruitful beings whose lives are healing for the world. They become trees of life. If we could learn the language of this river, we could begin already to live the vision of the new Jerusalem.

> *Merciful God, you have handed over your Word to us*
> > *and poured out your Spirit—your breath—upon us*
> > *as the source of your endless energy and love in our lives.*
> *Make us understand that the painful craving of our hearts*
> > *for meaning and for love and for life*
> > *is a gift.*
> *Lead us to the fountain of life that is your own life*
> > *flowing out to us*
> > *and let us see and hear and taste that it is true life.*
> *Teach us to live this mystery in ordinary places and familiar ways;*
> > *let us taste real life everywhere.*

A GARDEN EN- CLOSED

"The LORD God took the man and put him in the garden of Eden to till it and keep it" (Gen 2:15). God's initial idea was for humans to work in and enjoy a fruitful, well-ordered place. Tending the earth, the gardener brings forth fruit for nourishment and delight. Each day's work is a miracle of astonishment at the fruitfulness of nature. Something deep within each one of us still yearns for the peace and order suggested by the story of Adam's garden.

In addition to serenity, the garden suggests intimacy. "The man and his wife heard the sound of the LORD God . . . walking in the garden in the cool of the day" (Gen 3:8). The maker of creation, the Giver of all gifts, takes pleasure in the beauty that was made. Sheltered from our eyes, God remains present to us in the quiet of the garden—such is the imagery of the creation story. Our entering the garden is a symbolic re-entry into that unspoiled world.

One of the oldest instincts of human societies is to make gardens within the space of cities. Even though there may be farms just outside the city walls, ancient cities characteristically have a common, central plot of ground for meeting, for rest, and for reflection. Modern cities are rediscovering the importance of public gardens. It seems to be a need of our human nature to relax in a setting that evokes the quiet and the beauty of the countryside or of a token wilderness.

181

Monasteries and convents have their cloister gardens. This is an important symbolic element in monastic life which for ages has fostered a regime of silence (broken only for some true necessity). Therefore religious, walking through their cloister garden, were given symbolic contact with primordial mystery—with the creation story, with the presence of God in the world, and with the beauty of nature. Typically the cloister connected the monastic church with the residence of monks or nuns, with their chapter (or meeting) room, and with their refectory (or dining room). As a result, they circled the cloister garden many times a day, being reminded of the blessing of creation which God intended as a gift.

Monastic spirituality in the middle ages further elaborated the symbolism of the garden by making allusion to a beautiful but mysterious text in the Bible's Song of Songs. This strange poem is a love song expressing the passionate attachment of a prince (possibly King Solomon) to his favorite partner. Christians have from time immemorial allegorized this poem, seeing it as the expression of the love between Christ and the devout soul.

Here is a powerful image of intimacy and affection, placed on the lips of the prince (allegorically interpreted as a saying of Christ): "A garden enclosed is my sister, my bride, a garden locked, a fountain sealed" (Cant 4:12). Christ calls the Christian to secret closeness. In monastic life, centered on progress in prayer and a deeper relation to Christ, such a text takes on enormous weight. It becomes an image for the critical moment in the apprenticeship of prayer when interior silence becomes more eloquent than any words.

The discipline of prayer is, in fact, a work of friendship—a difficult friendship where attraction is strong, but where misunderstandings are inevitable. God lures the believer into a relation of love and devotion and invites growth in friendship and trust. But profound trust is difficult because God seeks to refashion the believer through the transformation of contemplative prayer. We enter the secret space of prayer—the garden enclosed—and suffer the awkwardness of any foreigner until at last the sense of the new language of silence breaks through.

Eastern Orthodox monasticism dealt with this same reality with a different but associated image. There someone learning contemplative prayer would be taught how to find the cave of the heart. There, in the silence of the heart, God can rest with us, teach us and guide us, console and heal us, using not the human language of words, but the divine language of stillness and love.

An ancient practice of Eastern monks has been to learn to coordinate breathing with prayer. By becoming consciously aware of the muscular activity associated with breathing, one also becomes sensitive to the analogy between breath and spirit. The "language" of breathing turns into a vehicle for inviting and welcoming the Holy Spirit.[30] Breathing in the name of Jesus, breathing out a prayer for mercy, one begins to create a habit of prayer that functions metaphorically as "the lungs of the spiritual life." Even without alert, focused attention, our breathing can eventually begin to take on the quality of ceaseless prayer, reflecting the systematic and conscious habit of prayer of the heart.

This prayer in the cave of the heart creates a great silence and a great peace within the one who prays. Such prayer also teaches the important lesson that it is not just the mind or the brain that prays, but the whole person—flesh and muscles and vital organs as well. The whole body-person is the temple of God, and the peace and well-being of the whole person is a prayer of adoration and thanksgiving.

The image of the garden enclosed is apt for this mystery of the prayer of the heart as well. It envisages a place of solitude where the most subtle movement of the Spirit will come to the fore. It mirrors the intense stillness of the soul who has learned God's language of eloquent silence where the deepest assurance of mutuality of love is simple presence.

In this context, the words of the Lord in the Book of Revelation take on touching beauty: "Listen! I am standing at the door, knocking; if you hear my voice and open the door, I will come in and eat with you, and you with me" (Rev 3:20).

Holy One, open our eyes to what you are doing:
   help us to understand.
Your words and your ways invite us to enter
   a new universe where everything is love and belonging.
You call us to be re-conformed
   to your simplicity, your peace, your goodness.
As you speak to our hearts
   in ''sighs too deep for words'' (Rom 8:26),
   re-tune our deepest instincts according to your own Spirit.
Make us trustful in the darkness of your visitation,
   peaceful in the silence of your love.

THE WORD OF GOD

"And the word became flesh and lived among us" (John 1:14). Here is a key to understanding God's idea for the Church. This powerful image from the opening section of John's Gospel suggests that Jesus speaks to the world not only when he is literally making utterances—preaching, teaching, and explaining—but also in what he is and in everything that he does. The Second Vatican Council's constitution on revelation teaches that Jesus perfected revelation "though his whole work of making himself present and manifesting himself: through his words and deeds, his signs and wonders, but especially through his death and glorious resurrection from the dead and final sending of the Spirit of truth."[31] In other words, Jesus' life is "word" in all these ways. His silence and his human wonder are word, as are his conversation and preaching.

We who believe that Jesus is God's word are also called to be a word of God that becomes flesh. This challenging theme is clear enough in sacred Scripture. There is a fascinating parallel between the gospel texts which speak of Jesus owning that his words come not from himself but from his Father and similar passages in which the disciples are told that, in times when their witness will be of greatest importance, it will not be themselves who speak, but the Spirit speaking in them.

So in John's Gospel we read: "For I have not spoken on my own, but the Father who sent me has himself given me a commandment about what to say and what to speak" (John 12:49). Compare this with Matthew, where Jesus says, "When they hand you over, do not worry about how you are to speak or what you are to say; for what you are to say will be given to you at that time; for it is not you who speak, but the Spirit of your Father speaking through you" (Matt 10:19-20). The word, then, both in Jesus and in believers, comes to utterance by the guidance of the Holy Spirit in moments when crucial words must be spoken on God's behalf.

Preachers learn that what affects their listeners is often not what they consider to be the wisest or most telling point in their sermons, but rather something else which touched their listeners' hearts for reasons altogether unclear. Likewise, friends in conversation discover that their sympathy and affectionate listening to the burdens of others have a power beyond anything they would have imagined. Cardinal Newman, the great nineteenth-century English theologian, took as his motto the Latin phrase, "Cor ad cor loquitur," which means "heart speaks to heart." Regarding God's word, the most powerful communication takes place at the level of the heart, not just with the exchange of words and phrases.

A haunting phrase of Jesus indicates another dynamic of the word: "You have already been cleansed by the word that I have spoken to you" (John 15:3). What is this cleansing? Jesus' word enlightens by teaching, empowers by forgiving, energizes by commanding, and excites by offering promise and vision. In our human friendships, a new level of intimacy is achieved when friends share secrets. Jesus' revelation about his life with the Father and the Spirit is such an offer of intimacy. It is meant to engage us in his apostolic dream, just as our sharing of intimacies with friends is an invitation to shared life. Perhaps another way of saying "You have been cleansed" is to say "You have been elevated—lifted up into a life of new meaning and new significance through the mysteries that I have shared with you."

The author of the Letter to the Hebrews also uses strange and intriguing language. "The word of God is living and active, sharper than any two-edged sword, piercing until it divides soul from spirit, joints from marrow; it is able to judge the thoughts and intentions of the heart'' (4:12). The word of God is living and active, that is to say, it enters into the ongoing processes of our reflection, our decisions, and our actions. Just as the Spirit acts within us in a way that is coordinated to our ordinary processes of living, so the word of God penetrates and enters into all of our feeling, thinking, speaking, and acting.

The image of the word as a sword prompts two ideas. A sword defends. At the end of the Epistle to the Ephesians, the writer tells us that we must put on the armor of God to be strong against the wiles of the devil. He counsels us to put on the ''sword of the spirit, which is the word of God'' (Eph 6:17). If we put God's word at the center of our vision of the world, we will be prepared to fight off understandings that are wrong and destructive. Another image of the sword, suggested by Hebrews' phrase, ''piercing until it divides soul from spirit,'' is that this instrument is, like a scalpel, sharp enough for a spiritual biopsy. The word cuts through confusion, just as a surgeon would cut away corruption in a wound. In this case, the divine agency of the word is more evident. God is alive in the word, even while the word resides in our memory, our imagination, and our quiet reflections.

In the First Letter of John, we read, ''The anointing that you received from [Christ] abides in you, and so you do not need anyone to teach you . . . as his anointing teaches you about all things, and is true'' (1 John 2:27). Merely hearing what is said in the preaching of the Church is not enough, according to this reading of 1 John; God's message must penetrate our hearts. This cannot happen except through the grace of the Holy Spirit, which is called here an ''anointing.'' Like the leaders of the early communities, we are called to be witnesses not only to the words that Jesus spoke, but to the life of the Spirit within us. Just as Paul wrote to Timothy, so we too are exhorted: ''Proclaim the message; be persistent whether the time is favorable or unfavorable: convince, rebuke, and encourage with the utmost patience in teaching'' (2 Tim 4:2).

The Holy Spirit gives the baptized a practical understanding of God's plan: ''[God] has both anointed us and marked us with his seal, giving us as pledge the Spirit in our hearts'' (2 Cor 1:22).[32] So the baptized are empowered to share in Christ's mission to bless, to instruct, and to influence the course of human events. Believers are called to bring newness of life to the events of their family and social life. They are called to be agents of renewal.

The point of our human living is to cooperate in realizing God's plan for the world. We alone can bring this plan to realization in our ordinary world, worked out in the routine of our day-to-day living. Pope John Paul II has challenged Christians to "restore creation to its original value";[33] this is another way of saying that we are called to participate in the transformation of culture to bring about an authentic vision of human well-being in a world of justice, peace, and communion in the Holy Spirit. This will call for an epidemic of benign contagion.

This mystery of the word, then, is not just a challenge for us to learn what God has said in the Scriptures, but a much deeper challenge for us to enter into a new and demanding ecology of thought, imagination, decision, and action. This word that is called the sword of the Spirit is meant to be a constitutive part of our humanity as believers, an endowment of our spiritual anthropology. This word is awake during our rest and our silences, active in our reflection and discernment, effective in our actions in cooperation with others. The word cuts through all our excuses about our unimportance or our impotence. To use the phrase of John's Gospel, God's word takes flesh in us and dwells in us. Yet if this reality is to have power and force in our lives, we must do all we can to learn and live the word. Read it, reflect on it, discuss it, celebrate it, and open our hearts to it. Then the sword of the spirit will both defend us and open for us the mysteries of God's love.

Your word is the path to life,
   the call that guides our hearts to freedom.
Open our eyes to perceive the meaning of your promise
   to share your life with us, O God.
Only when your teaching penetrates our thoughts
   and becomes one with our own vision of life

can we fully understand your deep love for us.
''Your word is a lamp to my feet
and a light to my path'' (Ps 119:105);
Give us, Holy One, joy in learning your purpose for the world
and delight in following your guidance.

ABOUT THE ARTIST

No one has had a greater influence on the development of American religious architecture and art in the past four decades than Frank Kacmarcik. He is a rare personality who possesses understanding, experience, and vision concerning every aspect of church design, furnishings, ritual space, and art. It is a tribute to his successful initiatives that others have followed in his footsteps as artist, designer, and consultant in the sacred arts, helping parishes and other communities to develop criteria for church building and renovation. In addition, for over forty years Kacmarcik has designed the covers for *Worship*, the American journal of liturgical studies. He seems to be an inexhaustible source of creative ideas.

Frank Kacmarcik was born on 15 March 1920, in St. Paul, Minnesota. Both his father and mother were devoted Catholics. Frank's father earned his living as an upholsterer and refinisher. Frank grew up in a family in which both the visual arts and music were part of ordinary family communication because singing and involvement in a variety of crafts were shared by them all.

After high school, Frank attended on scholarship the Minnesota College of Art and Design, where he cultivated a special love for painting and for graphic and book design. Later as a novice in St. John's Abbey in Collegeville in the 1940s, he became familiar with the paintings of Clement Fischauf, a monk who had been trained in the Beuronese school of religious art. Brother Clement became a devoted mentor, leading Frank to see himself as a disciple of this influential and important liturgical artist.

Frank left the monastery for the military in 1944 and served in the army in Europe during World War II. He functioned as a surgical technician in the U.S. Army Medical Corps and as chaplain's assistant. This experience in the military offered him many opportunities for travel and he became familiar with the cathedrals, monasteries, museums, and monuments of Western Europe—the largest treasury of Christian religious culture in the world.

After the war, Frank studied in Paris at the Académie de la Grande Chaumière, where he was trained in painting, and at the Centre d'Art Sacré, where he developed critical skills in religious art and church decoration. Once again, these years provided him with further opportunities to get a feel firsthand for the atmosphere and qualities of many of the Church's most beautiful religious buildings. He also began to assemble a remarkable collection of fine and rare books, manuscripts, and religious art objects. (This collection, at present at St. John's University in Minnesota, is one of the richest private collections of its kind anywhere in the United States.)

His characteristic style evolved during these years in Europe. One sees within his drawings as within his architectural plans his interest in woodcuts, old engravings, medieval manuscript illustrations, and Orthodox icons, as well as in contemporary painting and sculpture. One can also immediately identify anything that comes from the hand of Frank Kacmarcik because, if there is an eclecticism to his taste, it has become firmly rooted in a deep and original personal vision of his own. This is particularly true of his drawings.

In 1950, Frank returned to the United States and became a professor of art at St. John's University in Collegeville, Minnesota. In 1950, he began creating original art work for the covers of *Worship*, a responsibility which he continues to the present. In 1953, he collaborated with the famous German Bauhaus architect, Marcel Breuer, on the design and construction of the abbey church at St. John's—a building which has become a landmark of twentieth-century religious architecture. His stamp on this building and much else at St. John's could only have been placed by the active patronage of retired Abbot Baldwin Dworschak, O.S.B. Over the years, Frank has provided the abbey with a distinctive and beautiful repertory of logos for stationery, book designs, and identifying symbols. The headstones in the monastic cemetery are uniformly designed by his creative hand.

In 1955, Frank Kacmarcik moved to St. Paul, where he built a house and studio designed for him by his friend and colleague Breuer. When Breuer presented the plans for this house, he told him, "There is no bill. This is my way of telling you that St. John's Abbey church would not be as it is except for you." This characteristically lovely creation of Breuer's, a functional modernistic house fitted into a knoll overlooking the Mississsippi River, became Frank's refuge—a home, a library, a studio, and a hermitage all at once.

From this base, he worked as a full-time consultant in church design, printing, and the graphic arts. In addition to becoming one of the most influential voices in church design following the Second Vatican Council, he also designed for Benziger Brothers' publishing house many of the first generation of Catholic liturgical books in English in implementation of the council's call for a vernacular liturgy. In these books, he introduced a reform toward a simpler, more legible style. In this same period, Frank's stature was recognized by an invitation from the Royal Library of Sweden to be one of forty-three international typographers solicited to submit typographical designs for a Bible in honor of the five-hundredth anniversary of the Guttenberg Bible. He has been one of the strongest influences for nobility and beauty in objects serving Catholic worship in the three-and-a-half decades following the council.

Frank Kacmarcik is legendary among those who have the pleasure of his acquaintance for his trenchant criticism of artistic mediocrity. He has devoted his life to creating opportunities for ordinary people to find environments that might convert them to a more wholesome vision of religious beauty. Yet Frank is personally anything but pompous. He has said of himself: "I am a very ordinary person, born of

Slovak-Polish forebears. Had I been born in Europe, I would have begun life high in the Grand Tatra Mountains, would have become the official cowherder for the village of Landok, and probably would have been very happy.'' As Frank often acknowledges, he has been greatly blessed with gifts for identifying and creating beauty.

The drawings in this book represent part of the rich legacy of Frank Kacmarcik's ministry of visual catechesis. Each of these drawings is done in a style that is uniquely his own. The technique is called ''scratchboard drawing.'' It involves laying down an image in black india ink on a specially prepared drawing board that has a surface covered with gesso (a chalky white layer of paint). Once the black forms are in place, the artist then removes the dried india ink with a knife or scraper to allow the underlying layer of white to show through the black. This technique is similar in effect to woodcuts, but allows the artist greater flexibility of expression. He has a marvellously fluid line that creates a spirit of grace and naturalness in his work.

Frank was deeply affected by the work of the English engraver and type designer Eric Gill. Gill was an Englishman who devoted his life to creating fresh and original religious art. Like Gill's, Frank's drawings possess equal parts of discipline and fantasy. A glorious playfulness often shows up in these drawings. Yet the dramatic and captivating strength of his technique forces the viewer to ponder seriously the implications of the Christian mysteries that the drawings evoke.

These artworks resemble in spirit the music of the French composer Francis Poulenc. Poulenc was an important modernist who had a mid-life conversion to religious practice and who wrote some of the most beautiful and touching religious music of this century. Poulenc leads the listener through repeated episodes of bouyancy and melancholy, playfulness and high seriousness, sweetness and brashness— resolving the whole into a deeply moving sense of beauty and peace. As with Poulenc, the sincerity of Frank Kacmarcik's vision of a world shot through with grace is coupled with the authority of his artistic execution. This has allowed him to create images that are truly sacramental, that is, truly aids to understanding the presence of God in the world.

196

In 1981, the North American Academy of Liturgy offered Frank Kacmarcik its highest award to honor his distinguished contributions to liturgical renewal. The citation for the award reads as follows:

''For more than a quarter of a century, Frank Kacmarcik has served the churches of this country as a minister of visual environment. His work in graphics and in pioneering the role of artist-designer-consultant for church building, renovating and furnishing embodies commitment to high standards, freedom from fads, conviction that tradition lives, and remarkable correspondence with the best insights of a Church in process of renewal. With admiration and gratitude, in the month which completes his thirtieth year as cover designer for *Worship* magazine, the North American Academy of Liturgy presents its 1981 Berakah Award to Frank Kacmarcik.''

Later, in 1987, Frank was made an Honorary Member of the American Institute of Architects—one of seven persons selected that year ''in recognition of outstanding contributions to the architectural profession and to society as a whole . . . ; each has effectively promoted and enhanced quality in the built environment,'' according to the A.I.A. news release. He has been awarded more than sixty national and international awards in book design and the graphic arts, as well as numerous awards for building and renovation projects, including six coveted national A.I.A. awards.

In 1988, Frank asked to enter the monastic community at St. John's as a cloistered oblate and was accepted by Abbot Jerome Theisen. He now lives in the abbey as a member of the monastic community and continues his work of consultations and design in a small workroom at the back of The Liturgical Press. So much of the abbey bears the mark of his influence, that his moving in there has been a bit like coming home. Each day those in the monastery handle liturgical books imprinted with his logo for the abbey. One walks down corridors to find in many locations sculpture and other art objects found or commissioned for the abbey by Frank over many years. His Christian humanistic vision has become embodied in the environment of St. John's

Abbey in an exceptional way. It is both his home now and a home which he helped to make for his Benedictine brothers. This place is the greatest single contribution that Frank Kacmarcik has made to helping people see and believe.

In the 1950s, Frank asked Thomas Merton to compose for him a prayer for vocations to the sacred arts. This unusual composition is also a fitting description of his career. The Trappist monk sent the artist this prayer:

"Almighty God, Father of all light, Maker of the world, who has made us in your image, seers and makers: Look down into the abysmal darkness of our hearts and see the unutterable destitution into which our spirit and our art have fallen, since we have grown blind to the splendor of your truth. O Lord, who once heard the cry of Israel enslaved in Egypt, who delivered the people with great power and led them with your prophet Moses into the desert, send us now people of vision who will open our eyes once again to see your incorruptible light. O Lord, who showed to Moses on the flaming mountain the plan of a perfect tabernacle, in which a fitting worship could be offered to your majesty, send us chosen messengers and teachers, lovers of worship and art, who will restore with chaste and noble works the beauty of your house! May they teach us to see with pure hearts the splendor of your Son Jesus Christ and to express what we have seen in images worthy of so great a vision: through the same Jesus Christ, your Son, your Logos, your Art and your Splendor, in whom all things subsist and through whom, by the power of the Holy Spirit, all are called to be united with you forever. AMEN."

[For further reading about Frank Kacmarcik's career, see the following:

"Frank Kacmarcik—Berakah Award," *Worship* 55 (1981).

Robert Hovda, "The Amen Corner: Frank Kacmarcik—Art as Skill in Making," *Worship* 61 (1987) 358–64.

R. Kevin Seasoltz, O.S.B., "Living Stones Built on Christ" *Worship* 57 (1983) 115.

Robert L. Tuzik, "Frank Kacmarcik: Artist and Designer" in *How Firm a Foundation: Leaders of the Liturgical Movement*, R. L. Tuzik, ed. (Chicago: Liturgy Training Publications, 1990) 327–33.]

NOTES ON THE TEXT

1. See St. Thomas Aquinas, *Summa Theologiae*, vol. 2, *Existence and the Nature of God*, ed. Timothy McDermott, O.P. (New York: McGraw-Hill, 1963) 1.2, prologue, p. 3: "Concerning the nature of God, we must discuss first, whether there is a God, secondly, what manner of being he is, or better, what manner of being he is not. . . ."

2. Teilhard de Chardin, *The Divine Milieu* (New York: Harper & Row, 1965) 63.

3. See *Environment and Art in Catholic Worship: Bishops' Committee on the Liturgy* (Chicago: Liturgy Training Publications, 1986).

4. Gerhard Wehr, *An Illustrated Biography of C. G. Jung* (Boston and Shaftesbury: Shambala, 1989) 68. Jung's inscription was in Latin: "Vocatus atque non vocatus deus aderit"—a phrase taken from a collection of Latin aphorisms, this one a response of the oracle at Delphi.

5. Rudolf Otto, *The Idea of the Holy* (London: Oxford University Press, 1950).

6. See Aquinas, *Summa Theologiae*, vol. 1, *Christian Theology*, ed. Thomas Gilby, O.P. (New York: McGraw-Hill, 1963) appendix 1, "The Structure of the Summa," 43f.

7. Aquinas, *Summa Theologiae*, vol. 14, *Divine Government*, ed. T. C. O'Brien. See 1.103.1. ad 2; p. 7: ". . . even the permanent element would dissolve into nothingness, because it is from nothingness, unless it were sustained by the hand of God who governs . . ." and also 1.104.3; p. 49: ". . . [God] upholds [creatures] in existence in no other way than by the continuous bestowal of existence upon them. Therefore, just as before things existed God had the power of not giving them existence, and thus of not creating, so also once they are created he has the power of not continuing to uphold them in existence; then they would cease to be."

8. This point is treated at many places in Aquinas' writings, but for the sake of example see *Summa Theologiae*, vol. 2, *Existence and Nature of God*, ed. Timothy McDermott, O.P.; 1.3.4.c.

9. *The Documents of Vatican II*, Walter M. Abbott, S.J., and Joseph Gallagher, eds. (New York: America Press, 1966) "Constitution on the Sacred Liturgy" §8, 141-2.

10. ''A Hymn to Our Lady, from the Byzantine Liturgy of S. Basil'' in Donald Attwater, ed., *Prayers from the Eastern Liturgies* (London: Burns, Oates & Washbourne, 1931) 16.

11. Both a Greek text and an English translation are available in *The Acathistos Hymn*, G. G. Meersseman, O.P., ed. (Fribourg: The University Press, 1958) see 35f.

12. Citation from St. John Damascene, ''Second Homily on the Transfiguration'' (PG 96:564C), in Jean Corbon, *The Wellspring of Worship* (Mahwah, N.J.: Paulist Press, 1988) 60, 193.

13. *The Documents of Vatican II*, ''Dogmatic Constitution on the Church,'' §8, 24.

14. See *The Confessions of St. Augustine*, translated by E. M. Blaiklock (Nashville: Thomas Nelson, 1983), Book 3, Chapter 6, 65, which translates this passage as follows: ''But you [God] were deeper within me than my inmost being, higher than my highest.''

15. The clearest explanation of this theory can be found in Carl R. Rogers, *On Becoming a Person: A Therapist's View of Psychotherapy* (Boston: Houghton Mifflin, 1961).

16. St. John of the Cross, *Counsels and Maxims of the Spirit*, trans. John Rooney, M.H.M. (London: Catholic Truth Society, 1991) 16, §70: ''In this life's afternoon they will test you in love. Forget who you are and learn to love God the way he wants to be loved.''

17. *The Documents of Vatican II*, ''Dogmatic Constitution on the Church,'' §34, 60.

18. *Environment and Art in Catholic Worship* (Washington, D.C.: United States Catholic Conference, 1978) §34.

19. Ibid.

20. *The Rule of St. Benedict*, Timothy Fry, O.S.B., ed. (Collegeville, Minn.: The Liturgical Press, 1981) ch. 52, p. 255, and ch. 19, p. 215–16.

21. *Environment and Art in Catholic Worship*, §12.

22. *The Documents of Vatican II*, ''Constitution on the Sacred Liturgy,'' §102.

23. Ibid., ''Dogmatic Constitution on the Church,'' §11, 28–29.

24. Ibid., §40.

25. James Trefil, ''Dark Matter,'' *Smithsonian* 24:3 (June 1993) 27–35.

26. Bob Hurd, ''Angels,'' in Michael Downey, ed., *The New Dictionary of Catholic Spirituality* (Collegeville, Minn.: The Liturgical Press, 1993) 38-41.

27. While Hobbes' phrase became a slogan for a dog-eat-dog world, he himself hoped to reason toward a gentler, more cooperative society. For an explanation, see Paul Johnson, ''Hobbes and the Wolf Man,'' in J. G. van der Bend, ed., *Thomas Hobbes: His View of Man* (Amsterdam: Rodopi, 1982) 31f.

28. *Christifideles Laici: The Vocation and the Mission of the Lay Faithful in the Church and in the World* (Washington, D.C.: United States Catholic Conference, 1989) §34.

29. Cited in William H. Lazareth, ed., *Luther on the Christian Home* (Philadelphia: Muhlenberg Press, 1961) 95.

30. An excellent resource for understanding the Orthodox theology of prayer is *The Art of Prayer*, Timothy Ware, ed. (London: Faber and Faber, 1966) esp. the introduction, 9–38.

31. *The Documents of Vatican II,* "Dogmatic Constitution on Divine Revelation," §4, 113.

32. Text from *The New Jerusalem Bible* (Garden City, N.Y.: Doubleday, 1985).

33. *Christifideles Laici,* §14: "But in particular the lay faithful are called to restore to creation all its original value. In ordering creation to the authentic well-being of humanity in an activity governed by the life of grace, they share in the exercise of the power with which the Risen Christ draws all things to himself and subjects them along with himself to the Father, so that God might be everything to everyone (cf. 1 Cor 15:28; John 12:32)."

ACKNOWLEDGMENTS

I am indebted to many persons who have supported and encouraged my work on this book. Michael Naughton, O.S.B., director of The Liturgical Press, welcomed the project when it was little more than an idea in discussion. Kevin Seasoltz, O.S.B., editor of *Worship*, also gave much appreciated encouragement at the beginning.

A number of friends have devoted time and care to reading the manuscript and offering suggestions for its improvement. To Gerard S. Sloyan, Kathleen Norris, Joseph Gallagher, and Thomas F. O'Meara, O.P., I owe a singular gratitude for their detailed criticisms and recommendations. Ida Richard and Mark Wedig, O.P., read and commented on an early draft. Tilden Edwards, Director of the Shalem Institute of Spirituality, likewise reviewed the text and offered help for improving it. All of them generously contributed to the development of this book.

Gerard Austin, O.P., has guided and enriched my appreciation of the Church's liturgy for many years. He will find reflected here much that I first learned from our conversations.

I gratefully acknowledge the hospitality of the Institute for Ecumenical and Cultural Research at St. John's University in Collegeville, Minnesota, where much of this book was written. I express thanks to the Institute's director, Dr. Patrick Henry, and to his assistant, Sister Dolores Schuh, C.H.M., for their kindness during my Collegeville days. My sabbatical colleagues at the Ecumenical Institute, Patricia and Patout Burns, encouraged me many times with their unflagging interest in this project.

The University of Notre Dame allowed me a semester's leave in the spring of 1994 for which I am grateful. I note with pleasure the support and interest of my colleagues at the Institute for Church Life at Notre Dame.

Several of my Dominican confrères of the Southern Dominican Province have encouraged this book during its development. The work reflects as well, I think, the salubrious influence of Benedictine and Trappist communities where I have repeatedly received welcome and friendship over the years, especially the O + M Forest of Peace in Sand Springs, Oklahoma, the Trappist Abbey of New Melleray, Weston Priory, and St. John's Abbey. May this book be seen by them as a token of my sincere respect and appreciation.

The pioneering work earlier in this century of a handful of French Dominicans who collaborated on the revival of the arts in the Church and on the journal *L'Art Sacré* has long been an inspiration for me. It is a pleasure to remember here with gratitude Fr. Pie Régamey and the late Fr. Alain-M. Couturier. My love of the Church's liturgy and the arts has been inspired by their passionate commitment and courageous tenacity in the face of great hardships.

Tracy Blair, my secretary and assistant at Notre Dame, was patient and thorough in typing many revisions that succeeded one another over several months. Myriam Frebet, a member of the community of Les Dominicaines Missionaires des Campagnes, assisted in the organization of the chapters and provided inspiration and friendship as this project took shape. Sister Carole Kaucic, S.C.N., kept eager watch over the progress of the text and offered good suggestions and encouragement.

To my collaborator, Br. Frank Kacmarcik, I owe more than I can say. Our work together on this project was a pleasure for me. My wonder at his fertile religious imagination is a story of decades of delight. It is a joy to see this book appear in time to appropriately honor his seventy-fifth birthday. I offer my part in this project as a tribute to his great contributions to the life of the Church.

PPh

Seeing and Believing was written by Paul Philibert, O.P.,
and designed and illustrated by Frank Kacmarcik, Obl.S.B.
The text was set at The Liturgical Press in Palatino and Optima Bold,
typefaces designed by Herman Zapf. Sentinel Printing Company
printed the book on Weyerhaeuser Cougar Opaque paper; it was then
bound in Holliston Lexotone over board by Midwest Editions.

This is an edition of 1,500 copies, of which 375 are signed
by the author and the artist.

This book was completed on the Feast of Saint Andrew, 1995.